THE ORVIS

BEGINNER'S GUIDE TO

CARP FLIES

THE

ORVIS®

— BEGINNER'S GUIDE TO —

CARP FLIES

101 Patterns
&
How and
When to
Use Them

Dan C. Frasier

SKYHORSE PUBLISHING

Skyhorse Publishing books may be purchased in bulk at special discounts for sales promotion, corporate gifts, fund-raising, or educational purposes. Special editions can also be created to specifications. For details, contact the Special Sales Department, Skyhorse Publishing, 307 West 36th Street, 11th Floor, New York, NY 10018 or info@skyhorsepublishing.com.

Skyhorse® and Skyhorse Publishing® are registered trademarks of Skyhorse Publishing, Inc.®, a Delaware corporation.

Visit our website at www.skyhorsepublishing.com.

10 9 8 7 6 5 4 3 2

Library of Congress Cataloging-in-Publication Data is available on file.

Cover design by Adam Bozarth
Cover photo credit: Tuck Scott

ISBN: 978-1-62914-463-4
Ebook ISBN: 978-1-63220-080-8

Printed in China

Table of Contents

Acknowledgments

I WANT TO TAKE A SECOND TO THANK SO MANY PEOPLE without whom this book wouldn't have happened. First and foremost, I must thank Tom Rosenbauer, whose encouragement, guidance, and generosity made it possible. My daughter Ella, who at one time or another hated me doing this, loved me doing this, and wondered aloud about the lack of photos of her in the book. She sacrificed as much as anyone. My best friend Captain Tuck Scott was instrumental in both the fly photography and the collection and handling of the flies. It was like herding cats, and he did it brilliantly—thank you brother. McTage Tanner contributed incredible photography and acted as a sounding board. John Bartlett and Justin Watkins both listened, answered unending questions, and provided valuable feedback. Their influence runs throughout the book. And to all the people who contributed to the gorgeous photography: Brent Wilson, Cam Mortenson, Targhee Boss, Nolan Majcher, Adam Hope, Jim Pankiewicz, Mark Erdosy, Tim Creasy, and Will Rice, the book isn't the same without your photographs. And lastly, to all you fly tiers who submitted patterns. Thanks to you, I now have the greatest collection of carp flies ever assembled. Keep creating—you are redefining the sport.

Introduction

I KNOW YOU'VE BEEN TOLD THAT CATCHING A CARP ON the fly is like catching a permit blindfolded in 40-mph winds with a dull hook. Carp fly fishermen love to extol the difficulties in getting carp on the fly, and they aren't lying. It's not easy. Then again, we might have a tendency to make our own efforts appear a little more herculean than is actually the case. The fact is catching a carp with a fly is tough but not nearly as hard as you may have been led to believe. The real trick is picking the right fly and presenting it correctly. Carp won't eat the wrong fly, and they rarely make mistakes; it's why we seldom catch them inadvertently.

OK, bad news first. None of the patterns in this book are surefire bets the first time you hit the water. But now the good news: The magical carp fly that will get eaten consistently and even eagerly on your water probably does exist in these pages. When you match the right fly with the right water, the results can be incredible. You just have to figure out what the carp you are trying to catch are eating.

For many people, carp fishing involves putting aside preconceived notions.

Carp are probably the most adaptable feeders in North American freshwater. They have the ability to feed efficiently on almost every category of food items. When the most available and efficient food is baitfish, they are effective predators. If small nymphs are the most available food item, they are foragers. And if it's crayfish, they're something in between. Unfortunately for us, what is most abundant will vary from body of water to body of water and from month to month, meaning the food items that the carp is keyed on will change by season and body of water. In addition, even the best pattern will fail if it isn't mistaken for the preferred food item at that time and on that water. See? Simple.

Habitat, behavior, and even the scarring on their lips indicate what carp are eating.

Photo by Dan Frasier.

So the first and most important advice any book on carp flies can give is this: Find out what the carp are eating on the water you intend to fish. Kick over rocks, watch the fish's behavior, get muddy and wet—do whatever it takes to figure out what is the most available food item to the carp you are chasing. At the beginning of each part, I have described the indicators and carp behaviors when they are eating food items in this category. There will also be a discussion of the habitats that each prey prefers. When you can see feeding behavior that is consistent with a certain prey and you know that prey is abundant on that specific water, you can be pretty confident that you know which flies stand the best chance for success. Then and only then pick a pattern and go nuts.

How we present the fly to the fish is as important as fly selection. Presentation cannot convince a fish that the wrong fly is actually whatever they are eating. No matter how well you present a crayfish pattern to a fish that is eating midges, you aren't going to convince the fish that the crayfish is a midge. However, a poor presentation can talk a fish out of thinking that the right fly is actually food because the right fly with the wrong presentation will get refused just as readily as the wrong fly with the right presentation. When you understand what the carp are eating, you are able to identify what fly to show them. Understanding how that prey behaves, allows you to show the fly to them persuasively. For that reason, each category of fly will have a discussion of the behavior of the prey we are imitating and presentation techniques that match that behavior. Some of these presentations are tried and true on various other species of fish. Others are newly developed for carp. Don't be afraid to test presentations that you come up with yourself. This is a new arena in fly fishing, and it is evolving quickly.

Just continue to ask yourself, "How does this organism move just before a carp eats it, and how can I make my fly do the same thing?" If you keep those questions in your head, you will eventually find the presentation that works best for you.

Earlier I mentioned that carp diets vary wildly. Because of this variation in diet, a few important things will become obvious as you look through the flies in this book. First, the patterns are impressionistic rather than perfect imitations. Many of them could pass for items in different categories. Carp are intelligent fish. Give them the opportunity to convince

Photo by Mark Erdosy.

themselves that the fly is what they hope it is. Secondly, hybrid patterns can be very effective. If you make a fly that looks like it might be more than one type of food, you increase your odds. Lastly, the most important decision you will make in your carp fly selection is not the individual fly, but rather the category of food item. If you know the carp are eating nymphs, any number of the nymph patterns in this book may work. Having an understanding of which food the carp are eating answers the questions of fly size, profile, and presentation. If you have those three things right, the exact pattern you use will become a matter of fine-tuning. In other words, you'll already be catching lots of carp,

and finding the perfect pattern will only make it better. Thus, this book is separated by food item. Carp eat everything, but your carp only eat the category of everything most available to them. If you figure out that category, you are halfway home.

My final tip before we move onto the specific flies is about how all of this variation in diet

Photo by John "Montana" Bartlett.

by water, time of year, location on the water body, and time of day creates considerable uncertainty around fly fishing for carp. You are never quite sure if you are being refused because the fish have switched food items, or you are moving the fly wrong, you just aren't lucky enough that day. It is maddening to even the most seasoned carp fly angler. This uncertainty breeds a lack of confidence, and that is the worst thing someone targeting carp can bring to the water. Confidence, or faith, as a good buddy of mine puts it, is the most critical factor deciding success or failure on the water. Carp aren't going to telegraph to you that they have eaten your fly, they aren't going to hook themselves, and they will rarely give you the exact shot you desire. You need to make casts on faith that your skills and a little luck can get the fly where it needs to be. You need to set the hook on blind faith that it's time. The more carp you catch, the more often you will find yourself thinking, "I have no idea what made me decide that fly had been eaten." This is what makes being a beginning carp on the fly junkie so difficult. You can only develop the feel or intuition with experience, and that can't be taught. The best advice I can give is this. In order to speed the development of your carp sense, you have to catch a lot of

carp. The only way to catch a lot of carp is to cast to a lot of carp and set the hook a bunch. Casts and hook sets are free, so be confident in your abilities, your flies, and your budding intuition, and start setting the hook on the slightest movement. You'll quickly realize that you often can't see what's happening between your fly and the carp's mouth, and you can't hesitate to set the hook.

One last thought: The flies in this book are intended for common carp. While some will work on certain grass carp, many of them won't.

Set the hook early and often to build your intuition about when the fly has been eaten.

Photo by John "Montana" Bartlett.

Along with the physiological and behavioral differences between grass carp and common carp come large dietary differences. Grass carp are primarily herbivores. They are stocked for weed control purposes. An entirely different set of flies is required to consistently catch them, which is beyond the scope of this book. If it's grass carp flies you are after, you'd better just come over to my house, pour a scotch, and be prepared to hang out for a while.

PART

I

Meat

IF YOU READ ONE OF THE FEW BOOKS ON CARP, YOU'LL likely conclude that carp eat crayfish, and that is factually accurate. Some carp in some places do, in fact, eat crayfish, and it could be argued that this understanding is the genesis of carp fly design. Essentially, carp fly fishermen started with "carp eat crayfish" and built their way out. As time passed, designers realized that crayfish weren't the only organisms being eaten by carp and began to build flies accordingly. However, while they were venturing away from crayfish, they weren't abandoning this size of fly. Medium-sized prey are an important part of the diet of a carp on most water, and that size is where the focus of carp fly design remained for a long time.

Medium-sized flies can put very large fish in your net.

Photo by Mark Erdosy.

Photo by Dan Frasier.

These medium-sized flies represent the longest standing and most explored genre of flies for carp. It has grown to encompass more than just crayfish. Let's call it meat. Flies in the meat category range in size from about ¾–1½ inches long and attempt to look like one of the more meaty food organisms living in freshwater. Crayfish, worms, mussels, and clams all fall into this category.

As I said in the introduction, identifying what the carp are eating is the most important aspect to picking a fly. The best worm imitation won't catch a carp that is eating tiny nymphs. Thankfully there are a number of cues that the carp and the environment will give to anglers if the fish are eating flies in meat size range. The first thing to notice is how the fish are eating.

The quintessential carp-feeding scenario involves the carp with his head down and tail up, sometimes breaking the surface. Finding a fish in this position means you have found a feeding fish. That's a good start. It doesn't yet tell you what they are eating, unfortunately. That information is telegraphed in the carp's movements. Food organisms of the meat size are more able to flee or hide than smaller more help-less creatures.

Thus, the carp that are feeding on them will tend to exhibit more active movements. The higher calorie count of this larger prey makes them worth the effort. A tailing carp that will occasionally lunge forward or quickly turn its head is likely eating something you could call meat. If the fish are in very skinny water, you will see them picking or lunging their way around rocks or weed bases. These fish are not just feeding; they are hunting.

Tailing isn't the only cue that carp are looking for prey. Often they will be slowly cruising near the bottom. In this scenario, carp will be swimming along rather haphazardly and without obvious purpose.

Looking for carp tails is a good way to find feeding fish.
Photo by John "Montana" Bartlett.

Photo by Dan Frasier.

The sign that they are eating comes when they stop to pick something up, momentarily tailing or even changing direction to grab a fleeing food item. Once again, carp that are feeding on these larger food items will have to make pretty obvious movements to capture prey. They will work a little to get one of these larger food items.

One thing I can tell you for sure: to find fish eating organisms of this size, organisms of this size need to be present in the water. Obviously, each specific prey item will have a particular ecosystem that it likes best, and we will get into the specifics of those ecosystems as we get more in depth into each useful pattern. That said, there are some generalities that can be made concerning bodies of water that hold prey items of this size in abundance.

Good habitat for meaty prey tends to be relatively rich. Ponds, slow moving rivers, and lakes with a significant amount of life are prime

Photo by Aaron Smith.

homes for the majority of these animals. Rich, mucky bottoms, stands of weeds, and shallow areas all tend to hold larger prey items. While these animals are prey to carp, frequently they are predators themselves. They require an abundance of tiny bug life to feed upon. Weedy or mucky bottoms and rocky areas with significant moss growth are rich in the tiny bugs that baby crayfish eat.

Another consistent water feature is that they tend to be pretty shallow. Getting light to penetrate to the bottom is a key ingredient in supporting a body of water that is rich in plant

Aquatic life that falls into the meat category requires shallow, weedy, rich environments.

Photo by Jim Pankiewicz.

life and, therefore, small animal life. This is why flats are attractive areas to fly fish for carp. These shallow sections of larger water bodies see more light on the bottom than the deeper sections and thus hold more life. Carp will often move into these shallow areas to find the moderate-sized creatures that live there and eat them.

If it appears that the body of water can support abundant small animal life and that the carp feeding in the area are hunting their food, there is a pretty good chance the fly you select should fall into the meat category. Once you've gotten that far, it's time to dig a little deeper and decide which prey specifically to start with.

1
Crayfish

I HAVE A LOVE/HATE RELATIONSHIP WITH CRAYFISH. ON the one hand, they make up some of the most important flies in carp fishing because they are an integral part of the food chain in many carp fisheries. On the other hand, anatomically correct three-inch long crayfish patterns nearly ruined my early experiences in carp fishing. OK, "ruined" may be a little dramatic, but it sure felt that way at the time.

Photo by Targhee Boss.

When I first began fly fishing for carp, I did one thing right. I understood the importance of matching the hatch. So I went to the internet, and I asked it "What do carp eat?" The answer was loud and clear. They eat crayfish. Immediately, I rushed out and bought a few dozen of the best crayfish imitations I could find. All right, so I didn't rush out. I did it from my desk at home, probably in my underpants. Regardless, I ordered three dozen crayfish flies and went to work as soon as they arrived. These flies were three inches long, heavily weighted, and had all kinds of fancy material to recreate the shell, claws, and antennae. They looked really good to me. The fish hated them. The splash from the cast immediately spooked any fish in the area. If I got lucky and they didn't spook on the cast, they would as I quickly stripped the fly by their face. Crayfish are quick; better have quick strips, right? In the end, I never did get a fish to eat those big shiny crayfish. They would, however, eat a rust-colored Woolly Bugger if I moved it slowly enough. That got me thinking and looking around. Perhaps perfectly tied adult crayfish weren't the answer.

It was time I learned to better understand the crayfish. So I researched its life cycle. I learned that crayfish aren't all big, and they aren't always covered in a hard shell. Adult crayfish have a formidable appearance, but there are actually stages of life in which the crayfish is relatively vulnerable—times when a predator would want to key in on them. To best understand how to target carp that are eating this small crustacean, it pays to understand their life cycle and habitat.

Photo by John "Montana" Bartlett.

DESCRIPTION

Female crayfish are strangely caring in their mothering . . . well, as caring as a mudbug can be. After laying her eggs, the female crayfish will carry them around under her tail until they hatch. Even after hatching, the babies will stay under the mother's tail until they are ready to go out and hunt on their own. At that point, they are almost a half-inch long. Over the course of the coming year, these growing crayfish will molt up to eleven times by shedding their entire shell and slowly growing a roomier one. That's basically it. Egg, tiny baby, molt molt molt . . . adult. While alive, they tend to have rusts, oranges, olives, blues, browns, and blacks in them—crayfish are only a solid rusty red when they are in a steaming pile in the center of a table. This life cycle gives us some clues about how to tie and present a crayfish fly to a carp.

Like all carp fly fishing, carp won't eat a crayfish fly unless they are accustomed to eating real crayfish. This means understanding your body of water and the structure in the location you are fishing to know if crayfish are likely to be available.

Crayfish prefer bottoms with rocks and other structure large enough and piled so they can find small spaces to hide. It is important to their survival when they have molted their shell. It is also important because crayfish eat dead things and small living creatures, such as tadpoles, fish, and aquatic insects. Rocky areas, deadfalls, or significant weedbeds provide both ambush points and enough structure that small animals congregate around them. When you find carp working rocky areas, a

Rocks and plant life are important habitat features for crayfish.

Photo by Dan Frasier.

crayfish should be the first fly you think of.

Open mudflats or sand-bottomed areas are usually pretty poor habitats for crayfish. They prefer to not be exposed and lack the capability to bury themselves in the mud. Small crayfish patterns have been known to work in these situations because the patterns are suggestive rather than imitative and can easily be mistaken by a fish for an aquatic insect or even a dying baitfish. While crayfish can and do work in these situations at times, you will find far more success if you use a fly designed for these types of landscapes.

Crayfish also tend to prefer moving water. They are relatively sensitive to water chemistry and, therefore, don't withstand pollution very well. The flushing effect created by moving water helps ensure

Flowing water with numerous ambush points is ideal crayfish habitat.

Photo by Dan Frasier.

that there isn't a buildup of pollution. Carp can and do withstand polluted bodies of water quite well, so if you find you are fishing for carp in areas of stagnant water or with high pollution levels, crayfish patterns probably aren't the flies for you.

PATTERN CHARACTERISTICS

Effective crayfish patterns usually emulate the crustacean in the early part of its life. For starters, that means smaller than you think. Hook sizes 6 down to 10 tend to work well. The best patterns also focus on the periods of time when the crayfish has molted its old shell and is soft and helpless. These patterns are small and soft look-ing. They tend to leave off the claws altogether, but if they don't, the claws are also made of a soft and supple material. Most carp crayfish flies inte-grate the same list of colors I already mentioned: rusts, oranges, olives, browns, and blues are all important colors. Frequently peaches, yellows,

Crayfish patterns fished to carp feeding around riprap can be extremely effective. Photo by Anna Swanson.

and pinks can also be effective because crayfish that have molted their shells have a tendency to be a little lighter in color.

PRESENTATION

The ideal fish to throw a crayfish pattern to is sometimes referred to as a shopper. That is to say, the fish is slowly working along the bottom looking for meaty morsels. Early on it's easy to confuse this behavior with fish that are cruising and not eating, but as you do it more and more, the differences will become obvious. First of all, the carp will be moving along rather slowly and with no obvious destination. Their swimming pattern will look random. Secondly, they will stop and dip down or lunge forward rather frequently. What is happening is that the carp is moving along looking for something substantial to eat. When it sees a crayfish that is exposed enough to get at, the carp will pounce rather quickly on the little crustacean. These shopping carp are great targets with a crayfish fly. However, finding fish that are actively feeding on the bottom isn't enough. The structure should also indicate that the fish may be actively feeding on small crayfish. That means, the fish should be picking around structure or over rocks.

A less ideal but still serviceable target is a fish that is tailing consistently and moving slowly. These fish are rooting for something buried in the bottom, and crayfish don't do that. That said, many times an opportunistic carp will accept an easy meal. For the most part, fish exhibiting this behavior are on larger flats with less structure, but if they happen to be around rocky outcroppings or along the edges of weedbeds, a crayfish pattern may work. If they aren't near structure, they are looking for something else and will be much less likely to eat

Photo by John "Montana" Bartlett.

your crayfish. Just know that if you are consistently fishing to carp showing this heavy tailing behavior, you will have better luck with different flies.

The idea is to give the carp the easiest meal possible. A small molted crayfish is both slow moving and helpless—an easy target. They have softer tails and are simply trying to get into a nook or cranny and wait until their shell reforms. Your presentation should exhibit this behavior. The Drag-and-Drop presentation can be extremely effective in this situation.

The Drag-and-Drop is a presentation method that I haven't ever heard used anywhere but in carp fishing. The idea is simple. Carp eat things that are easy to grab, so make the fly easy to get.

The Drag-and-Drop works best when you have good control over your fly, which means a short line. First you have to stalk close to the fish. Once you are as close as you can get, you cast beyond the fish by a few feet. As soon as the fly is on the water, you lift your rod tip to slide your fly along the surface of the water, manipulating it so it is directly above the fish's dinner plate. Once there, you let the fly fall straight down in front of the fish. No strips, no tugs, no pops. Just drop it dead on his dinner plate. Carp will frequently slide either slightly up or forward to grab the fly as it descends presumably mistaking it for a spooked crayfish trying to flee to the structure.

When using the Drag-and-Drop presentation, it's important to know exactly where your fly is in relation to the fish. You are presenting the fly

Using the drag-and-drop presentation requires stealth to get within range of your target.
Photo by John "Montana" Bartlett.

directly into the feeding zone and setting the hook when the carp moves to eat it. Because the fly is so directly presented, the takes will be subtle. It could be a simple flair of the gills, or you'll see the lips extend. Since the fish will move very little to eat your fly, you must take extra care to determine when the fish in on your fly.

When the Drag-and-Drop isn't an option, there are other presentations that can work well. A cast right at a carp will spook it. These fish are not aggressive. You must let them find the fly rather than the fly finding them. Casting just beyond or in front of the fish and letting the fly settle to the bottom is a good idea. As the carp

Photo by Kiley Boss.

approaches the fly, slow strips are the order of the day, and a slow crawl away from a feeding fish can be particularly effective. Because they are crawling along the bottom, these flies are usually tied hook point up to avoid snagging. Watch closely for the take, as it can be pretty subtle, and then hang on!

FLY PATTERNS

Barry's Carp Fly—Barry Reynolds

Hook: Tiemco 200R #6
Thread: UTC 60 Orange
Eyes: Black Lead Eyes 5/32
Nose/Tail: Brown Rabbit
Body: Rusty Brown Crawdub
Back: Brown Scud or Shell Back
Rib: Brown Fine Wire
Collar/Legs: Rusty Brown Hen Hackle

Photo by McTage Tanner.

Befus Swimming Carp Fly—Brad Befus

Hook: Tiemco 200R size 6–12
Thread: UTC 140 color to match fly color
Weight: Lead wire in front half of hook
Tail: Rabbit underfur dubbing
Abdomen: Rabbit fur dubbing
Wing case: Mottled Brown Medallion Sheeting
Thorax: Rabbit fur dubbing in a dubbing loop
Legs: Pumpkin silo legs

Photo by McTage Tanner.

Roughdub Crayfish—Christopher Vargo

Hook: Dai-Riki #930 size 8–4
Eye: Medium, large, xl bead chain or lead eyes
Claws: Two small clumps of squirrel tail (not stacked) positioned and post wrapped at least once

Photo by McTage Tanner.

Body: Dubbing blend with ¼"–½" cut squirrel tail, mixed 50/50 with your favorite dubbing

Carp Crack—Jean Paul Lipton

Hook: 1X Strong Straight Eye
  O'Shaugnessy (stainless), Mustad 34007,
  or Umpqua U401, size 8
Thread: UNI-Thread 6/0, Fire Orange
Tail: Medium MFC Centipede legs, Hot
  Orange
Body: Roughfisher's custom spectral seal
  sub dubbing, Burnt Orange

Photo by McTage Tanner.

Thorax: Ruffed Grouse (or Hungarian
  Partridge or India Hen), dark/brown; Roughfisher's custom
  spectral seal sub dubbing, Burnt Orange
Head: #8 (4.0 mm or 5/32") Bead chain, black

Backstabber—Jay Zimmerman

Hook: Gamakatsu SL45, size 6
Thread: UNI-Thread 6/0, tan
Weight: ⅛" Dazl-Eye, gold
Body: Dave Whitlock SLF, Red Fox Squirrel
  Nymph Abdomen
Wing: Burnt Orange Marabou
Hackle: Natural Mottled Brown India Hen
  back

Photo by Tuck Scott.

Primordial Carp Stew—McTage Tanner

Hook: Gamakatsu SL-45, size 8
Thread: 140 denier Ultra Thread, black
Eyes: ⅛" Spirit River Dazzle Eyes, black
Weight: 8 wraps of .025" lead
Body: Swisher's Rub-A-Dub in a dubbing
  loop, olive
Collar: Whitlock's SLF dubbing, squirrel
Tail: 4 splayed flexi-floss strands, light olive
Belly: 4 flexi-floss strands, light olive
Beard: Rabbit, olive variant

Photo by McTage Tanner.

Pike's Carpy Charlie—Matt Pike

Hook: Umpqua U401 size 8
Thread: 6/0 UNI Rust Brown
Weight: Lead Eyes/Micro/Black
Body and Thorax: Custom blended dubbing (4 parts Hareline HD15: 4 parts HD01: 1 part HD4: 1 part ICE187)
Rib: Yellow Stretch Magic (any small vinyl rib)
Legs: Olive Hungarian Partridge
Wing: Orange Antron Yarn

Photo by Tuck Scott.

Legion of Doom—Justin Watkins

Hook: #4–8 hook, #6 best all around
Thread: 6/0 or 8/0
Tail: Tuft of Marabou
Rib: Small wire
Shellback: Clump of peacock herl
Underbody: Chenille, usually drab color
Hackle: Grizzly, usually reds or blacks
Eyes: Dumbbell eyes of about any finish, weighted to match hook size and desired sink rate

Photo by Tuck Scott.

Tiger Paw—Jim Pankiewicz

Thread: Black
Hook: Tiemco 5262 size 8
Eyes: Lead dumbbell eyes size XS or S
Tail: Orange rabbit fur striped with a Sharpie
Body: Orange rabbit fur striped with a Sharpie
Legs: Round black rubber, medium

Photo by McTage Tanner.

Carp Bitters—Barry Reynolds

Hook: Gama SL-45, #6
Thread: To match (orange, olive, rust)
   UTC 60
Eyes: Medium black bead chain
Nose/Tail: Barred Mini Marabou to
   match (orange, olive, rust)
Legs: Barred Sili-Legs to match
   (orange, olive, rust)
Body: Crawdub to match (orange,
   olive, rust)
Collar: Hen hackle to match (orange,
   olive, rust)
Weight: 10–12 wraps .020 lead-free
   wire

Photo by McTage Tanner.

Pikes Egg Bitter—Matt Pike

Hook: Vintage Mustad, or #4 Carp
   Pro gaper
Thread: UNI 6/0 orange
Weight and Eyes: Wapsi micro lead
   eyes/CCG
Body: Shaggy's dub (orange), UV Ice
   dub (orange), Elk and Deer body
   hair mixed, Egg Yarn

Photo by McTage Tanner.

Befus Wiggle Bug

Hook: Tiemco 200R, 3XL, #8–12
Thread: Brown
Tail: Brown Bugskin, trimmed to
   V-shape
Rib: 4X tippet material
Body: Dubbed Rusty Brown rabbit fur
Legs: Mottled Brown Hen saddle
   hackle

Photo by McTage Tanner.

Gregg's Bitter Bugger—Gregg Martin

Hook: Dai Riki 810, 930, or equivalent, size #6

Head: Medium bead chain, red-coated with 15-minute epoxy colored with cheap nail polish bright to dark red

Thread: UTC 70 Denier or equivalent wine or burgundy red

Weight: 7–8 wraps .025" lead snug to head

Photo by Tuck Scott.

Tail: Fur from wine, leech red, burgundy, Zonker strip with guard hairs removed

Rib: Small copper or red wire wound through hackle

Appendages: MFC Sexi Legs, red

Hackle: Red Dyed Saddle tied at head

Body: Wapsi Squirrel SLF Spikey Dubbing, Rusty Brown head to tail and back

Primordial Crust— McTage Tanner

Hook: Tiemco 760SP, size 4

Thread: 140 denier Ultra Thread, black

Eyes: 5/32" Spirit River Dazzle Eyes, black

Weight: 15 wraps of .025" lead

Body: Swisher's Rub-A-Dub in a dubbing loop, rust

Tail: 4 splayed buggy nymph legs, brown

Belly: 6 MFC Speckled Sexy Legs, orange

Photo by McTage Tanner.

Wing: Zonker strip pierced by the hook at the back and tied in at the front

Jannsen's Wizard Sleeve—Zach Jannsen

Hook: TMC 811S, size 6 or 8
Weight: Medium red dumbell eyes
Tail: Two 1" sections of gray Flexi-Floss
Body: Sowbug SowScud dubbing
Claws: Two clumps of olive rabbit fur to extend to the bend of the hook
Collar: Whiting Hen Saddle Lt Olive then Whiting Hen Saddle Olive Grizzly

Photo by Tuck Scott.

Gregg's Muskrat Wiggler—Gregg Martin

Hook: Dai Riki 810, 930, or equivalent #6
Eyes: 5/32" Dazzle Eyes, 2–3 eye lengths behind eye
Weight: 7–8 wraps .025" lead wire behind eyes
Thread: UTC 140 denier, black or equivalent
Tail: Root beer Marabou, other colors may be used
Carapace: Peacock herl, 12–16 strands
Rib: Small red or copper wire
Body: Muskrat fur cut from hide and inserted into 5" dubbing loop, picked out well after ribbing, fur trimmed flat on bottom

Photo by McTage Tanner.

Erdosy's Carp Crab—Mark Erdosy

Thread: Danville Denier 70 match color of fly
Hook: Gamakatsu Stinger Sizes 2–6
Eyes: Lead Dumbbell Eyes Medium/Large, should be plated—nothing shiny
Legs: Speckled/Barred Rubber Legs, such as Montana Fly Company Speckled Sexi Legs
Dubbing: Just a small base layer of your favorite dubbing
Body: Brown UV Polar Chenille
Hackle: Long Webby Schlappen
Wire: Gold, Copper, strap to secure Schlappen
Back: Thin Skin (bottom), Stripped Magnum Rabbit Fur (top)

Photo by McTage Tanner.

Cohen's Carpantula—Pat Cohen

Hook: Gamakatsu L10-2H
Eyes: Small Lead Dumbell
Tail and Body: EP Silky Fibers Tan
Rib: Ultra Wire Hot Yellow, medium
Wing Case: EP Silky Fibers coated
     with CCG Hydro
Legs: EP Tarantula Brush Tan

Photo by McTage Tanner.

Foxy Lady—Dan Frasier

Hook: CarpPro Gaper size 6–8
Eyes: Bead chain or lead eyes
     depending on required sink rate
Collar: Red Fox Tail
Body: Rust-colored dubbing
Tail: Red fox tail tied over Silly Leggs

Photo by McTage Tanner.

Pike's The Force—Matt Pike

Hook: Umpqua U401 #8
Thread: UTC, 140, Fl. Orange
Weight and Eyes: Gold Spirit River
     Dazl-eyes, 3/32"
Tail: Natural Hungarian
     Partridge
Body: Hareline #4 hare's ear,
     hd4
Rubber legs: Olive
Thorax: Hareline wiggle dub
     #178 natural
Collar: Natural Hungarian
     Partridge
Overwing: Ep streamer brush,
     111sb 03 rust

Photo by McTage Tanner.

Catch's UV2 Carp Leggs Crayfish— Eric Beebe

Hook: Dai-Riki #810, size 4
Tail: Barred and Speckled Red Crazy Legs
Body: Black UV2 Dubbing
Neck: Black Schlappen
Throat: MFC Red Barred Ostrich Herl
Eyes: Dazzle Dumbbell Eyes
Beard: Black Schlappen
Thread: 210 Denier Black Danville

Photo by Tuck Scott.

2

Worms

EVERY LIVE BAIT DEALER KNOWS THAT WORMS ARE AN important staple in the diet of any fish. Bait fishermen throughout the country use everything from night crawlers to wax worms to catch countless species of fish. The worm is no stranger to spin fishermen either, as an entire cottage industry has developed around the soft plastic worm in its multitude of forms. Put simply, the worm is one of the foundations of all types of fishing.

I grew up fishing night crawlers under bobbers or on the bottom. An important part of the let's-go-fishing ritual was the stop at the bait shop to get a Styrofoam container jammed with big juicy worms. I learned how to break them in half, the best way to put them on the hook, and remember clearly that feeling of dread as the worm supply dwindled when the bluegill were still biting.

Worm patterns are a very important component of a carp fly fisherman's arsenal.

Photo by Brent Wilson.

With all of that experience in the effectiveness of worms, you'd think I would have immediately embraced worm flies as something important. Unfortunately for me, I didn't. As I took up fly fishing, it was like I had finally graduated from the worm. I turned to traditional fly patterns without giving worms a second thought. Sure, I carried a few San Juan worms and they worked, but they certainly weren't my go-to flies. I was relying on the flies that had been created by the generations before me, and I assumed that the lack of worm flies was an indication that they weren't important.

Despite the fact that both aquatic and terrestrial worms are abundant in most bodies of water in the United States and their effectiveness in other forms of fishing, relatively few worm flies exist in traditional fly-fishing patterns. The San Juan worm

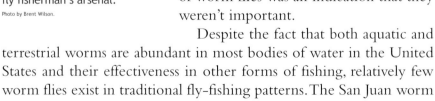

is the obvious exception, but it leaves much to be desired. It lacks movement in the water and is not durable, among other problems. Beyond the San Juan, there just aren't many worm flies to choose from.

There seems to be a stigma that surrounds worm flies that make them something of a last resort to trout fly fishermen. I've heard guides refer to using a worm fly as bait fishing and have talked to a few that didn't think worms were a naturally occurring food source for trout. Strange, considering how many worms live in the water. Fortunately for us, people who fly fish for carp aren't afraid of a little stigma. Sometimes I think we relish it.

DESCRIPTION

More than 22,000 aquatic and terrestrial worm species are known to science. They live in all marine environments and moist soils and take on about every coloration and size you can imagine. Additionally, the larval stages of many insects are very wormlike in appearance, while not technically being worms. Everything from midge larvae to caterpillars are in this wormlike group.

Photo by John "Montana" Bartlett.

Aquatic worms live out their entire lives in the water. They burrow in soft mud and sandy soils or live under rocks, deadfalls, and other structures. From here, they are sometimes washed into currents or dislodged by rooting fish, making them vulnerable to predation.

Terrestrial worms require moist soil to live. That means that many of them live near bodies of water, making them available to fish on a relatively frequent basis. They can blunder into water or be washed in by rains or runoff. They actually serve an important role in a carp's diet. Much like flood tide redfish or bonefish, carp like to work their way up into shallow water during floods. The ground here is usually not underwater; as the water rises, it slowly

Carp will frequently move into flooded areas to gorge on worms.

Photo by John "Montana" Bartlett.

covers soil that holds a bunch of bug life, including worms. Carp move up into the flooded area and gorge on the influx of bug life forced out of the ground as the water covers the land. In instances such as these, worms are extremely important flies.

PATTERN CHARACTERISTICS

Carp fly designers have been busy at work designing a number of worm flies that address all of the shortcomings of the traditional patterns: natural movement in the water, improving the sink direction to keep the hook point up, and varying sink rates for different water speed conditions. With these improvements, the new worm flies take more fish.

The new worm patterns incorporate a number of characteristics that make the fly better than a piece of chenille tied on a hook. They range from very small to two inches in length and include materials that are bulkier than chenille and exhibit far more motion in the water. Worms wiggle underwater, and your fly should, too. Many of the new patterns are tied to land hook point up, so they can be presented on the bottom to a fish without constant snagging. Reds remain the most prevalent color in worm flies, but some tiers are beginning to use browns and tans to better match the colors of the worms available to the carp in their waters. This becomes a fine line to tread. You want your fly to be highly visible to the fish so they can see and eat it. On the other hand, most natural prey have camouflage for exactly the same reason. You will have to use trial and error to find out what worm colors work best for you.

The new generation of worm flies is opening up an entirely new genre of food items to imitate. That may not be the most important thing they have done, however. Later we will see how they are redefining the concept of flies created for carp. But for now, let's focus on fishing a worm fly as it is.

PRESENTATION

Presentation for this style of flies is not as simple as it might seem. Some of the flies are designed to dead drift in current, rolling along the bottom or drifting in the current into the feeding zone. Others are weighted heavily and intended to stand on their head like a worm burrowing into the bottom. These flies should be presented as delicately as possible and left to stand while the fish works up to them. They can even be slowly stripped to give the impression of swimming, although very little movement is usually the order of the day. Deciding which fly and which presentation method to use depends on the behavior of the fish you are targeting and the water you are fishing.

Carp exhibit two very different behaviors that suggest the use of worm flies. As you look through the patterns, you'll notice that some flies are obviously designed for one scenario and some for the other. This makes worms hard to categorize. The first behavior is a slow, steady tailing in mud, sand, or gravel. This fish has its head down and is rooting hard in the soft bottom looking for the worms that live there. When the carp are feeding this way, they will usually stir the water up

Mud plumes in the water are surefire signs that carp are feeding. Worm patterns can be great in these situations.
Photo by Brent Wilson.

enough to make a mud cloud. These plumes of mud in the water can be a good indication to fishermen that carp are present and feeding.

These fish are in still water or slow-moving backwaters. Worms predominantly live in silty or soft bottoms, so a strong current that scours the sediment off the bottom is something to avoid. In that case, the best worm flies are the larger, heavier flies.

The second situation where worm flies are effective is when you find carp holding in a current and eating like a nymphing trout. Worms will dislodge and wash into feeding lanes quite frequently. In this situation, carp will frequently take a small worm pattern that is drifted into their feeding zone. When casting to these fish, be sure to use the smaller, lighter flies so you are able to get a dead drift in the current.

Either way, subtlety is the name of the game with these flies. The new materials being used will give your fly a significant amount of lifelike movement without requiring that the angler move the fly. Let the fly do the work. It is better to let the carp stumble upon a helpless worm than require the fish to chase something that is swimming away.

FLY PATTERNS

McTage's Leather Trouser Worm—McTage Tanner

Hook: Tiemco 2457 caddis, size 8
Thread: UTC waxed 280, red
Bead: 3.25 mm tungsten, black
Eyes: #6 bead chain, stainless
Body: 15 or 20 lb Amnesia Running Line, red
Tail: Zonker strip with hair trimmed to 1/8" long and tapered at the end, red
Head Cement: Loon Outdoors UV Knot-Sense (optional)

Photo by McTage Tanner.

Foam Trouser Worm—McTage Tanner

Hook: CarpPro Gaper, size 6
Thread: UTC waxed 280, red
Bead: 3.25 mm brass, black
Eyes: #6 bead chain, stainless
Body: 15 or 20 lb Amnesia Running Line, red
Head Cement: Loon Outdoors UV Knot-Sense (optional)
Tail assembled from:
Fourteen 1/16" thick, 1/8" diameter foam plugs made with a hole punch, dark red.
Uni big fly thread (B), red
Spirit River extra small glass bead, black
2.7mm brass bead, black
Loon Outdoors UV Knot-Sense

Photo by McTage Tanner.

Carp Assassin—Jean Paul Lipton

Hook: 2X strong curved, e.g. Scorpion Venom 2X, size 8
Thread: UNI-thread 6/0, Red
Weight: 3/16" Bead, Tungsten, or Brass
Body: Micro Chenille, Red
Rib: Ultra Wire Medium, Red
Gills: Marabou, Red; Krystal Flash, UV Pearl

Photo by McTage Tanner.

Worm Cluster—As tied by Gregg Martin

Hook: Mustad C67S #8, Dai Riki 135 #8, or equivalent
Eyes: White medium bead chain ¼–½ hook shank length, or to match body
Thread: UTC 70 denier or equivalent, white or to match body
Body: Three 2" strands white vernille or micro vernille, tied at bend, looped to head, slightly singed

Photo by McTage Tanner.

Vladi Worm—Chris Galvin

Hook: Owner Mosquito 1/0 (or Gamakatsu Split Shot/Drop Shot 1/0)
Underbody 1: Twelve to fourteen wraps of .015 lead at bend
Underbody 2: Red Floss
Overbody: Crown Condom strip (cut ½–¾" and wrapped 2x or 3x over floss)
Rib: 4x mono or mono thread
Head: 50 GSP Orange and Cyanoacrylate for durability

Photo by McTage Tanner.

Watkin's FYI—Justin Watkins

Hook: #4–6 short shanked
Thread: 6/0 or 8/0 to match size
Tail: Two strands of chenille twisted together and folded in half
Body: One of the chenille strands wrapped forward
Eyes: Dumbbell eyes to match hook and desired sink rate

Photo by Tuck Scott.

Maggot Cluster—Pat Cohen

Hook: Mustad C49S size 8
Thread: Danvilles Flat Waxed Nylon 210, White
Maggots: Ultra Chenille Standard White, slightly singed

Photo by Tuck Scott.

Hammond's Fuzzy Worm—Travis Hammond

Hook: Size 8 or 10 scud hook
Weight: Nickel-black tungsten bead in 5/32
Thread: Match to color of chenille
Body: Orange, brown, olive, or pink ultra standard chenille
Hackle: Size 16 grizzly dry fly hackle

Photo by Tuck Scott.

Jan's Carp Tickler—Orvis

Hook: Size 8 Caddis hook
Thread: Red
Eyes: Small bead chain
Tail Tip: Red Marabou attached with wrapped thread and superglue
Tail: Red Micro chenille
Body: Red cactus chenille
Legs: Nymph silly legs

Photo by McTage Tanner.

3
Clams and Mussels

THE FIRST TIME I TARGETED CARP THAT WERE FEEDING on mussels, I couldn't figure out what the hell was going on. The water clarity was excellent in the shallows, and the high sun and light wind made seeing the fish easy. I'd managed to stalk well within casting range and present the fly to numerous fish. Most spooked as soon as the fly moved. The rest would work up to the fly and then seemingly flee for no reason. I had carp in front of me, they were tailing, and the pockmarks all over the bottom let me know it wasn't the first time. The silt bottom looked like flyover footage of World War II carpet bombing, with softball-sized holes everywhere.

These fish were clearly players. I was showing them proven flies at close range, and I couldn't buy an eat. After an hour of frustration I walked, or rather slinked, away, glad that I was alone. Eventually I would return to this spot and spend more time observing and less time casting. What I noticed were the crushed shells of mussels littering

Softball-sized pockmarks in the silt are a good indication that the carp are feeding on clams and mussels.

Photo by John "Montana" Bartlett.

the bottom. Now it all made sense. The carp were there to graze on a bed of mussels not chase down a fleeing crayfish.

Freshwater mussels and clams are an important part of most food webs. Their ability to filter feed serves to clean waterways of floating debris and their large numbers make them an important protein source for many animal species, including carp. Matching the hatch is always an important aspect of fly fishing, and nowhere is that more true than in fly fishing for carp. Understanding the importance and prevalence of these shelled snacks to carp's diets can be the difference between catching fish and occasionally picking one up now and then.

Most aquatic ecosystems contain clams and mussels that carp depend on as a food source.

Photo by Mark Erdosy.

Because they exist in so many bodies of water, bivalves can become a primary food source for carp almost anywhere. Check the water you are fishing. If you see crushed shells strewn about the bottom or potholes where carp have repeatedly dug food out of the bottom, bivalves may be an important forage source for the carp there.

DESCRIPTION

Clams and mussels are widely distributed filter feeders in North America. The majority of their lives are spent sitting still and feeding on nutrients they filter from the water. They like to bury themselves in soft bottoms, such as mud, sand, or gravel, and feed by sticking a straw-like apparatus up and into the water above them.

Knowing the life cycle of a clam or mussel is important when trying to imitate them. It can tell us a lot about the sizes that are preferred by the fish, as well as the habitats that support the bivalves in large numbers. That, and it's a little creepy.

A female mussel expels a bunch of eggs that have been fertilized by her catching drifting sperm that was released into the water by males. These fertilized eggs then float along looking for a host fish in order to attach to the gills or fins. There, the baby clams will extract oxygen from the host fish until they reach a size to support themselves. After

Mussels and clams are more abundant in smaller sizes.

Photo by Dan Frasier.

living on the fish as a microscopic parasite for a short while, the tiny mussels drop off and bury themselves in the benthos. From there, they live out their lives filtering water through their valves.

Clams and mussels can be found in sizes ranging from nearly microscopic to as large as a small saucer. They exist in a variety of colors to camouflage themselves as rocks or hide in mud, but for the most part they are mottled browns, blacks, and grays. The most visible feature of a buried clam or mussel is the siphon. This is the tubelike structure that protrudes from the muck to filter water. Commonly, this is assumed to be a part of the foot of the clam, but that isn't technically correct. It is, however, attached to the foot and is usually the same color. The foot and siphon are fleshy and normally range from a pale gray or light yellow to faded pink.

There is one important signal for an angler to determine if the carp are primarily eating clams. I've mentioned earlier the crushed clam

Photo by McTage Tanner.

shells. When a carp takes in a clam or mussel, they move it back to the pharyngeal jaw deep in their throats and crush it. Once crushed, they discard the shell pieces and eat the flesh. These discarded shell pieces will often shine very white on the bottom. The opalescent inner surface of the shell will be exposed, making the pieces quite

Carp feeding on clams and mussels can leave the bottom littered with iridescent shell fragments. Look for this as an indication of clam-eating carp.
Photo by John "Montana" Bartlett.

visible. If the bottom you are fishing is littered with these broken shells, you are on the right track.

PATTERN CHARACTERISTICS

The first important thing to remember is that mussels exist in sizes smaller than we are used to seeing them. These things start really tiny, and that is when they are most susceptible to predation by carp. Carp have a pharyngeal jaw—basically a crushing device in the back of their throats that allows them to crush the shells of creatures such as mussels quite easily. That said, research suggests that these jaws are most efficient on items that are the size of the carp's eyeball or smaller, and your imitations should be a similar size.

Knowing how these animals live also gives us a good idea of what particular characteristics a fly needs to emulate them. The coloration of a clam or mussel imitation is usually a mishmash of browns, blacks, and olives. But the clam isn't just lying on the bottom in its shell. It is probably buried in the mud with a fleshy-toned siphon (the straw apparatus) sticking out and filter feeding. This is why many clam flies will have flesh-toned parts incorporated or even extending from the fly, to appear as a slightly open clam with a siphon pointing up.

PRESENTATION

Carp will come upon clams and mussels by rooting around on the bottom of a body of water, taking in rocks, sticks, and anything else they come across. Their highly developed tongues and mouth structures, along with

Carp tailing in gravely bottoms may be eating clams.
Photo by Tim Creasy.

an amazing sense of taste, will allow them to quickly sort the food from the non-food and spit out anything unappetizing. Carp find and eat clams and mussels with heavy tailing and rooting in gravelly or soft bottoms. They won't have to move quickly or chase anything to get a real clam, so they shouldn't have to do that to eat your fly either. This telltale behavior is the best indicator that they are feeding on clams. This is a different behavior than the shopping they do for crayfish.

The way carp feed on bivalves makes fishing these flies incredibly easy and extremely difficult. Presentation is easy: Put your fly in front of a fish that is working along the bottom. If the fish is taking in and

Photo by Dan Frasier.

expelling items in the search for food, your fly will be one of the items they take in. Please don't strip a mussel fly; it's hard to sit still, but please. Seriously. The hard part is detecting the take. You have about a half a second between a fish taking in your fly and expelling it, during which you have to set the hook. You will have very little cue as to when the fly has been taken. Know where your fly is. When the fish gives you any indication it is testing an item, such as lips extend-

ing, gills flaring, or head turning, then set up. If you miss the set, just recast and try again.

FLY PATTERNS

Darth Clam—Jean Paul Lipton

Hook: 2X strong curved, e.g. Scorpion Venom 2X, size 8
Thread: UNI-thread 6/0, Brown
Weight: 6mm gunmetal bead
Body: Furry Foam, Olive
Siphon: Ultra Chenille, Claret
Foot: Antron/Zelon, Amber
Head: Pearl Glitter epoxy

Photo by McTage Tanner.

Majcher's Clam—Nolan Majcher

Hook: Daiichi 1120 size 12–16
Bead: 1/8" black
Thread: 6/0 red UNI-thread
Body: Glo Bug Yarn, egg
Tail: Ultra Chenille (red, tan, orange, brown)

Photo by McTage Tanner.

Hammond's Soft Clam—Travis Hammond

Hook: Size 8 or 10 scud hook
Weight: Size 5/32" tungsten bead ahead of small black bead chain eyes
Thread: Brown
Body: Brown Free Range dubbing or Swishers Rub-a-dub in brown
Foot (tail): Red, pink, or Claret Ultra standard chenille
Hackle: Brown Hen Hackle over brown CDC

Photo by McTage Tanner.

Mr. P's Carp Carrot—Jim Pankewicz

Thread: Black
Hook: Tiemco 3769 sizes 6–10
Eyes: Nickel colored brass size 7/64, 1/8, 5/32 (primarily 1/8)
Tail: White or black round rubber, medium
Body: Rust or Orange dubbing
Hackle: Pheasant rump dyed yellow

Photo by McTage Tanner.

Catch's Clam—Eric Beebee

Hook: Dai-Riki #810, size 4
Tail: Standard Pink Ultra Chenille
Body: Hareline Pre-Colored adhesive Crab Coins (super glued together)
Eyes: Standard Lead Dumbbell Eyes
Thread: 210 Denier Pink Danville

Photo by McTage Tanner.

PART

II

Nymphs

THE FIRST CARP EVER CAUGHT ON A FLY ROD PROBA-bly ate a nymph pattern. Small traditional nymphs have been used for years to target carp with immense success. As the sport has evolved, other genres of flies have emerged, and some have seemed to overtake traditional nymph patterns in popularity. In certain cases that makes sense. Specialty flies can be successful on specialty fish, but nymphs still have an important place in the carp angler's fly box. In most situations on most bodies of water, a carp will eat a properly-presented nymph. If I were dropped from a plane into parts unknown and told I had to catch carp to live, I'd bring a big box of nymphs.

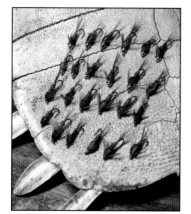

Traditional trout nymphs are very effective carp patterns.

Photo by Dan Frasier.

There are two major characteristics of nymph patterns that make them such useful carp flies: versatility and delicacy. Anglers can present nymphs in such a wide variety of ways and represent so many different food items that you will rarely find a fish that is impossible to take on a nymph. Tailing carp routinely flush nymphs out of the mud and are more than happy to eat one that is falling onto their dinner plate. The same goes for slowly cruising fish. A nymph pattern in a slow dead drift to the bottom or with a gentle stripping action can draw a strike. Carp feeding right along the shore will take a small dapped nymph, and even sunning fish have been known to eat a nymph that is suspended in front of them.

The nymph's versatility doesn't stop at addressing differing carp behaviors. Situational differences can render some flies useless but nymphs the least so. Fish in still water can be presented with a nymph by allowing

Dapping nymphs to fish feeding right along the bank can be a very effective tactic.

Photo by McTage Tanner.

the nymph to drift to the bottom immediately in front of the fish. In heavy current, high-stick nymphing for carp can be extremely effective, and a dead drift on a slow-moving river into a fish's feeding zone also works well. Sight fishing in clear water is a great way to present a nymph to a carp, but that isn't always available. When the water is turbid or the fish are deep, you can fish nymphs with strike indicators and cast to bubble trails or other disturbances made by fish. In short, an adaptable angler and a versatile nymph make almost all carp fishing situations manageable.

The delicacy of most nymph patterns is the other characteristic that makes them so effective. Carp are notorious for spooking off of flies, even when they are properly presented. Weighted patterns, such as the heavier meat patterns, will spook carp that are not looking for items that big. I don't know whether they find them threatening or are simply startled by seeing something unexpectedly larger than what they are eating, but they will run from one. Nymphs, on the other hand, are small enough that even when the carp doesn't eat the fly it will rarely flee. That means more shots per fish.

The delicacy of small nymphs also allows the angler to get away with less-than-perfect casting without blowing a school of fish. Weighted flies splat on the water. When they are cast too close to a fish, that splat will cause the fish to flee. Nymphs are smaller and lighter. They tend to land softer on the water, allowing the angler to not have to lead a fish as far. If the angler does put the fly too close to the fish, the lighter landing and unobtrusiveness of nymphs results in fewer spooks.

It's not all easy casts and multiple fish days with nymphs. These small flies do present some significant challenges to a carp angler. Detecting a take is always a difficult process when fly fishing for carp; they are subtle eaters and never more so than when eating nymphs. The small size of the bugs makes it inefficient for the carp to move very far for a fly. This limits how well a take is telegraphed to the angler. The easiest way to combat this situation is to know where your fly is in relation to the fish, and set the hook when the carp works up on your nymph. Of course, the size and subtle colors of many nymphs makes seeing them in the water nearly impossible, which complicates the process of knowing where your fly sits on the bottom.

If you do manage to get a take and a hook set, an entirely different problem presents itself. You may now have a twenty-pound fish on a size 12 nymph hook. I can't tell you how many hooks I have broken or straightened. Most of the time it's during the set that the hook opens. It then eventually works itself out during the fight. If you find this to be a consistent problem, try using a lighter rod. I will go down from my seven-weight rod to a five-weight when I am fishing tiny flies. I need the more forgiving tip of the lighter rod to help protect my hook. What I give up in authority to fight a fish is probably not as much as you think. The pull strength of a fly fishing setup is defined by the tippet strength not the rod weight. More importantly, the added authority of a heavier rod is useless after it straightens your hook.

Big carp can straighten even big hooks. Small nymph hooks are particularly vulnerable.

Photo by John "Montana" Bartlett.

The versatility of nymph patterns is due to the prevalence of nymphal stage insects in all bodies of water. Nymphs make up the base forage layer for almost every water body that sustains life. Many nymphs are herbivores, and the ones that aren't tend to prey upon other tiny insects that are. That means plant life and algae are important indicators of how dense nymph populations will be on a given body or section of a body of water. Carp living in rich habitats are selective about fly size and profile. When fishing areas that appear rich in plant life, keep in mind that the carp may be attuned to eating particular nymphs to the near exclusion of all else.

Traditional trout nymphs work well when targeting carp, but they do have some shortcomings that needed to be addressed. Fly designers have modified many trout patterns to more adequately deal with some of the situations encountered by carp fly fishermen, such as the warm or still water where carp often live, resulting in two distinct

Areas rich in aquatic plant life can produce carp that feed exclusively on nymphs.
Photo by Tim Creasy.

groups of carp flies. The first are traditional patterns or modifications on traditional patterns. These flies are probably recognizable to most fly fishermen. The second group consists of damselfly and dragonfly nymphs. These flies are great for addressing carp that are hard to target with more traditional patterns. Both groups are important. Let's first look at the more traditional patterns.

4
Traditional Nymphs

I MENTIONED THAT THE FIRST CARP WERE PROBABLY caught on traditional trout nymphs. Well there is no probably about my first go-to carp fly, a size 12 golden stonefly nymph. There were no golden stoneflies in the water I was fishing, and to tell the truth, I can't even recall why I owned those flies. That will tell you just how frustrated I had become by carp—I was chucking my last resort at them.

I had been fishing for carp for nearly two years when I stumbled upon how well nymph patterns could work. It was a high water year that spring. A favorite river of mine was running relatively swiftly for a little meandering prairie river, and the carp were fat and happy. All of the crayfish patterns in the world wouldn't interest them. Part of the problem was the difficulty I was having presenting a crayfish to a fish in that swift water. Most of the fish I found were holding in traditional nymph spots: the soft water behind a rock or a seam where food was being conveyed directly to them. My crayfish patterns were weighted, which meant I couldn't get the current to carry them to the fish. A presentation directly in front of the fish was difficult. The obstacles that the fish were holding behind made a slow crawl in front of the carp impossible. When I did manage a good crawl in front of a carp's face, they just weren't interested. Obviously I had to change something.

I remember clearly the individual fish that showed me what I was doing wrong. It was holding directly behind a rock in quick current. I watched the fish for a while, and the wink of its white mouth and flash of its side as it rolled on something told me it was eating. It looked like a submarine and fed like a nymphing brown trout. I wanted that fish so badly.

The previous two hours had been spent throwing meat patterns at fish that were tailing in a mucky backwater and coming up empty. Given this fish's location, I couldn't even picture a way to get a weighted crayfish to him. So I went to my fly box and found the biggest, buggiest flies I could find that I thought could ride in the current. I took up a position where I could cast upstream and across and let the fly drift directly in front of the rock. It was my hope that it would find its way into the flow and around. I made the cast and a slight mend; the fly slid just around the rock, and the carp just turned and ate it—simple as that.

I went on to catch four more fish that evening—a personal best at the time. I caught fish that were tailing, one that was cruising slowly, and another one eating in the current. Clearly, I'd solved carp fly fishing forever. It only took a month for the fish to change what they were eating and a week after that for me to begrudgingly put away the stonefly nymph. It's always hard to retire a favorite fly for the season.

DESCRIPTION

Nymphs is a category too broad to describe all of the characteristics of the animals the fly imitates. Some nymphs look like tiny cockroaches while others look almost wormlike. Some are carnivores and others are herbivores. Nymphs run the gamut of underwater insects. There are a few things that most of the animals have in common, however.

One characteristic that a majority of insects in their nymphal stages embody is that they are small. Nymphs on most water are no larger than one half inch long with a vast majority being far smaller than that. It never ceases to amaze me that a large fish can be caught on such a small food offering. There are two factors that make this work.

The first is the nymphs must be plentiful and available. Most bodies of water hold nymphs of some sort, but just having them in the water isn't enough. A large quantity of nymphs is required to sustain a carp population. Once again, you are looking for water that is pretty rich. Mucky or weedy bottoms can be good nymph habitat, as

Nymph imitations can be deadly when the real things are abundant.

Photo by Jim Pankiewicz.

are riffles and other structures that provide protection from the current and plant life for the nymph to graze on. These characteristics of the water body indicate that enough nymphal insects may live there to attract the carps' attention.

The second factor that allows tiny bugs to feed large fish is the calories-in versus calories-out ratio. Carp are only able to take in enough nymphs to sustain themselves if they don't have to work very hard doing it. Luckily for the carp—not so much for the nymphs—their size leaves them pretty helpless when in open water. A good current can dislodge nymphs and leave them tumbling. A carp that has positioned itself to take in these bugs without needing to move far can gorge itself without expending much energy. In still water, the logic is the same. If a carp happens upon a nymph that it can eat with little effort, it will do so. If the fish has to move much, it's not worth the effort.

PATTERN CHARACTERISTICS

You're probably already familiar with traditional nymph patterns. However, there are a few things that help make these flies translate to carp. Most of the time, using flies that are on the larger end of the nymph spectrum will increase your level of success. Carp are quite opportunistic, and we aren't too concerned with matching the hatch exactly—just the general prey category. That is to say if they want nymphs you better give them nymphs, but they aren't counting the legs or measuring the tail-to-torso ratio. With that in mind, nymphs in the size 12, 14, or 16 range tend to work. They are big enough to garner some attention but still small enough to look like an aquatic insect. Add to that the pull strength of even a medium-sized carp and you'll want all the hook you can get away with. Some tiers will go as far as making the flies up to a size 6. If you can make that work you should, but if the carp, is refusing your fly, get smaller. When fishing nymphs to carp, you are bound to straighten a few hooks, but tipping the scales a little further in your favor can make a difference.

Most of these flies will also be lightly weighted. A small bead head can help to get the fly down into a fish's feeding zone, but too much weight will prevent a good dead drift. Subtlety, like with most carp flies, is important here, too. Fists full of rubber legs, flash, or even shiny beads can spook carp. Nymphs aren't going to attract a fish. They just need to look attractive to a fish that happens upon them.

PRESENTATION

The most popular way to present nymphs is the dead drift: a fly cast into the current upstream of the fish, and then allowed to drift help-lessly along. The idea is to imitate a nymph that has become dislodged from its hiding place and is tumbling downstream. Nymphing for trout is commonly held out as the most effective way to catch fish. The same can be said of fishing for carp that are feeding in a current. Just remem-ber that the fish isn't going to move far for a nymph, so the drift should put the fly directly into the fish's face.

Still water situations call for a different presentation. The lack of current means drifting the fly to the fish is impossible. Instead, attempt to have the fly fall directly in front of the fish. The Drag-and-Drop method of presentation discussed earlier can be a great way to accom-plish this. The fly looks like a nymph diving for cover, and the carp want to catch them before they can hide. Casting beyond a fish and dragging the fly into the fish's feeding zone can also be a good way to put the fly directly in front of the fish. Just remember, the fly should look helpless by the time the fish finds it. Let the fly lie motionless by the time the fish happens upon it.

The traditional nymph can also be a fantastic way to address stillwa-ter fish that are too deep or in water too turbid for good visual cues. Attach a strike indicator to your leader far enough up that the nymph will suspend just off the bottom. Cast in front of the bubble trails that carp create when rooting along the bottom or in front of mud clouds that the carp are kicking up. Watch the indicator as the fish approaches, and set the hook on the slightest movement. The fish will have eaten the fly more often than you might expect.

FLY PATTERNS

Jim's Carp Hare's Ear—Jim Pankiewicz

Photo by McTage Tanner.

Thread: Black
Hook: Tiemco 3769 #10
Bead: Copper or brass 3/32
Tail: Comparadun deer hair
Rib: Gold or silver tinsel
Body: Gray dubbing
Legs: Round white rubber—medium

Gregg's Carp Hare's Ear—Gregg Martin

Photo by McTage Tanner.

Hook: Dai Riki 070, TMC 3761, size #10, or equivalent
Eyes: 1/8" Dazzle Eye, 2 eye lengths behind hook eye
Thread: Brown or tan UTC 70 denier or equivalent
Weight: .025" lead wire, 3/16" flattened behind eye
Tail: Cascade Crest Micro Sili legs, white barred black
Rib: Small copper wire
Abdomen: Hares ear or mask blended with like color antron, or similar coarse dubbing, picked out well
Wing Case: 12-14 strands of peacock herl
Legs: Same as tail
Thorax: Same as abdomen or Wapsi Squirrel SLF Spikey Dubbing natural, grey squirrel

Bead Head Hare's Ear—Orvis

Weight: Tungsten Bead
Hook: 3X-long nymph hook (here, a Dai Riki 285), sizes 12–20
Bead: Gold, 7/64-inch

Weight: .015" lead-free round wire
Adhesive: Zap-A-Gap
Thread: Olive, 6/0
Rib: Gold Ultra Wire, brassie size
Tail: 10-12 pheasant tail fibers
Wingcase: Tinsel mylar flat pearl
Abdomen and Thorax: Hair's mask
    and rabbit-fur dubbing, mixed

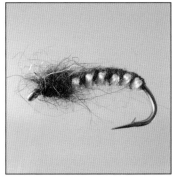

Photo by Tuck Scott.

Ty Weave Nymph—Ty Goodwin

Hook: Mustad 3906, sizes 6–10
Thread: 6/0 in color of choice
Abdomen: DMC 25 embroidery
    thread in colors of choice, typically a
    light color is used for the underbody
    and a darker hue for the back
Thorax: Dark coarse dubbing, brushed
    to flare the dubbing fibers
Weight: .15" lead wire

Photo by McTage Tanner.

Bead Head Zug Bug—Orvis

Hook: 2X-long nymph hook (e.g. Dai
    Riki #730), sizes 14–16
Bead: Gold, 7/64-inch
Thread: Black, 6/0
Tails: Peacock herl
Rib: Silver tinsel
Body: Peacock herl
Wing case: Mallard or wood duck flank
    feather
Legs: Hen hackle
Head: Tying thread

Photo by Tuck Scott.

Gregg's Scud—Gregg Martin

Hook: Mustad C67S #10

Thread: UTC 70 Denier brown, tan, or equivalent

Body: Wapsi Squirrel SLF Spikey Dubbing, natural fox squirrel, dubbed front to bend and back, well picked out

Weight: (Optional) .025 lead as keel on top length of body

Photo by Tuck Scott.

Gregg's Upside-Down Red Fox Squirrel Nymph—Gregg Martin

Hook: Dai Riki 280, size 8

Bead: 3/16" Tungsten Bead

Thread: Brown, burnt orange, or tan UTC 70 denier or equivalent

Keel: 3/8" length of .022"–.023" flattened mono, tail abuts keel

Tail: Clump fox squirrel back near tail with long guard hairs

Photo by McTage Tanner.

Rib: Extra fine oval gold tinsel

Abdomen: Fox squirrel belly blended with like-colored antron (earth ombre or ginger) dubbed front to tail and back

Thorax: Fox squirrel back blended with like-colored antron

Legs: Sili Legs, pumpkin black flake

Hackle: Speckled hen back, similar soft hackles

Gregg's Hookup Clouser Swimming Nymph—Gregg Martin

Hook: Dai Riki 810, 930, or equivalent, size 6

Eyes: 5/32" Dazzle Eyes

Weight: 7-8 wraps of .025" lead wire behind eyes, tail abuts lead

Over Tail: Clump of olive hare's mask

Tail: Olive dyed pine squirrel zonker strip, 3/4"

Abdomen: Olive hare's ear mask or ear, blended with like-colored antron or coarse fur equivalent, dubbed front to rear and back, picked out

Wing Case: 12-16 strands Peacock Herl

Hackle: Webby saddle, Schlappen, grizzly dyed olive

Thorax: Same as abdomen

Photo by McTage Tanner.

Mean Ole Dirty Frisco—Ty Goodwin

Hook: Mustad 3906, sizes 6–10

Thread: Black 6/0

Tail: Black hackle fibers

Abdomen: Coarse black dubbing, such as Awesome Possum

Rib: Medium green wire

Thorax: Black SLF Prism dubbing

Wing case: Black Swiss Straw

Hackle: Purple dyed guinea feather

Photo by Tuck Scott.

Carp Swallow—Chris Galvin

Hook: Gamakakatsu SL45, size 6

Thread: Tan UTC 70

Tail: Hen Pheasant Marabou

Abdomen: 80% Hares Mask, 20% Clear (white) Antron

Rib: SM gold wire

Hackle: Pheasant Rump

Collar: SLF Fox Squirrel Thorax Dubbing

Bead: 3.2 mm Tarnished Gold Tungsten

Photo by Tuck Scott.

Egan's Headstand—Lance Egan

Hook: Tiemco 2457, sizes 6–10
Thread: Tan 6/0
Tail: Rabbit
Body: Rabbit dubbing
Hackle: Brown rooster
Eyes: Silver bead chain
Legs: Pumpkin Sili Legs
Collar: Peacock sword
Head: Antron dubbing

Photo by McTage Tanner.

Black Betty—Jim Pankiewicz

Thread: Black
Hook: Tiemco 3769, sizes 6–10
Eyes: Nickel-colored brass 7/64", 1/8",
    5/32" (primarily 1/8")
Tail: Red round rubber, medium
Body: Two strands of peacock herl
Rib: Gold wire, counter ribbed
Hackle: Pheasant rump dyed black

Photo by Tuck Scott.

Chocolate Cherry—Jim Pankiewicz

Thread: Black
Hook: Tiemco 3761, sizes 6–10
Eyes: Nickel-colored brass dumbbell
    7/64", 1/8", or 5/32" (primarily 1/8")
Tail: White round rubber, medium
Body: Brown chenille, medium
Hackle: Red grizzly saddle hackle
    wrapped liberally

Photo by McTage Tanner.

5
Damsels and Dragons

DAMSELFLIES AND DRAGONFLIES ARE PREVALENT IN many rich warm and cold water environments. We've all seen them in their adult form flying around and freaking out people who think their long tails are stingers.

In their nymphal stage, these bugs can represent an important staple, even a primary item, in a carp's diet. Their abundance and size make them a good option for hungry carp. That is one reason these flies are quickly becoming an important fly pattern but not the only one. The nature of these bugs, namely their tendency to swim in open water, allow anglers to use these flies to catch fish they previously considered poor targets.

Photo by Dan Frasier.

Fish swimming in open water, often called mid-column fish, have traditionally been viewed as difficult to take on a fly. Sinking flies move through the fish's strike zone too quickly to be eaten, and a carp will rarely rise for a floating fly unless they are already feeding on the surface. Being predators, damselfly and dragonfly nymphs are active swimmers that move up and down the water column. They rely on their ability to move to chase down prey. This behavior makes them a natural target for fish that are in the middle of the water column and willing to eat. The flies that imitate

Dragonfly and Damselfly nymphs allow anglers to target fish that were previously thought poor targets.

Photo by Adam Hope.

these active swimmers often have a slow sink rate, which allows them to be nearly suspended in the water directly in front of a carp. The unique behavior of these bugs defines fly design and presentation.

DESCRIPTION

Underwater vegetation plays an important role in the bug's life. During reproduction, female adults often lay their eggs on or near underwater vegetation. The nymphs of these two bugs will commonly spend most of the early stage of life in shallow water where there is an abundance of plant life. The plants provide protection and feeding opportunities for these carnivorous nymphs. Being carnivores, these nymphs will hunt and ambush smaller prey items for food, and beginning life near vegetation helps ensure the availability of smaller prey.

As the nymphs mature, they will venture away and can be found swimming in more open water. They are serious predators and will hunt for smaller aquatic insects, tadpoles, or even small fish. Eventually the nymphs will migrate to vegetation when preparing to emerge. As they become adults, damselflies and dragonflies crawl out of the water on plants. Once they are out of the water, they spread and dry their wings to take flight. It is in this adult stage that we normally see them. The adult insects are also voracious predators. They can live for months in this adult stage eating winged insects they capture in the air. Eventually the female will lay her eggs in the water and die.

Damselfly and Dragonfly nymphs begin their lives on aquatic vegetation.

Photo by Tim Creasy.

Damselfly and dragonfly nymphs are predominantly olive, dark brown, or black in coloration, although they can be found in light tan or an almost faded yellow color. In the nymphal stages, these bugs range in size from just millimeters to nearly an inch in length. They are relatively slender bugs with segmented bodies and long prominent tails. Perhaps the most distinguishing feature of these bugs is the size and shape of the head. Both dragonflies and damselflies rely on sight as they feed and have oversized eyes set on the sides of their relatively wide heads. These prominent eyes give the nymphs extraordinary vision.

PATTERN CHARACTERISTICS

Flies that imitate damsel and dragonfly nymphs tend to range from ¾ to 1 inch long. They are usually tied on long-shank, light-wire hooks to balance the need to imitate their long, slender bodies and maintain an appropriate weight for a slow drift to the bottom.

The coloration for most damselfly and dragonfly nymphs ranges from light yellow to a dark olive or brown and can sometimes incorporate various other colors, giving a mottled appearance. Many patterns incorporate some kind of shellback to replicate the nymphs' hard shells and allow for easier segmentation of the body, and the tail materials display movement in the water. A damselfly or dragonfly nymph is a capable swimmer. The real thing wiggles its tail furiously to propel itself. Materials such as marabou work well to give the flies the wiggly tail action exhibited by the real nymph.

The most important feature in these flies is that they are rarely weighted. Damselflies spend their lives swimming and hunting rather than crawling on the bottom. Most presentations will require that the fly doesn't descend through the water column too quickly. It's important that these flies are tied with enough parachuting materials to slow the descent and offset the natural weight of the hook.

PRESENTATION

The nature of the bugs and design of these flies allow for some interesting presentation opportunities. Remember, part of the allure of these flies is that they can be presented to fish that are in the middle of the water column. That is a unique situation and it requires some unique presentations. The most effective presentation is closely related to the Drag-and-Drop we discussed earlier in the book. Basically, you are getting the fly past the fish and pulling it into position. The fly is then allowed to slowly sink to right in front of the carp. Once there, the fly can hang in the water and wait to be eaten, or you can swim it in tiny slow strips away from the fish as though the fly were fleeing. The slowly sinking fly will look like a nymph diving for cover and require the fish to follow it down a little to eat it. The fleeing fly will induce the fish to speed up and catch it. Both methods are highly effective.

These presentations are unique, effective, and quickly becoming a favorite among carp anglers. The reason being that it allows fish previously thought to be poor targets to become more likely hookup candidates. Carp that are slowly cruising or hanging mid-column are extremely difficult to catch with a traditional weighted pattern. The fish are rarely willing to move far enough to eat a fly on the bottom when they aren't actively feeding there already. Thus, it was thought that these mid-column fish were virtually uncatchable. With the advent of these lightly weighted and slow-sinking nymphs, an angler is able to have a fly drift slowly through the water column and into the fish's feeding zone where it can be easily eaten. The parachute effect created by the tying materials and slow sink to the bottom of a weightless fly leaves it hanging in the feeding zone long enough to attract the attention of the carp, oftentimes drawing a strike. This technique opens up a huge number of opportunities.

Cruising or mid-column fish aren't the only good targets for damselflies and dragonflies. Tailing and rooting fish are always good targets, and these unweighted flies can even be used when current isn't a consideration. When a carp is tailing and feeding on the bottom, it will frequently scare aquatic insects as it goes. These nymphs flee for cover, which can mean diving to get back into the benthos. Some of the more violent takes that a carp angler can experience are by allowing one of these lightly weighted flies to slowly drift to the bottom just in front of a feeding carp. The fish will oftentimes lift off the bottom or rush forward to catch the nymph before it escapes.

FLY PATTERNS

Vargo Rabbit Tail Dragon— Christopher Vargo

Hook: Dai Riki # 930, size 6

Eye: Typically XL bead chain or lead eyes

Body: Dubbing of your choice

Tail: Rabbit strip

Throat and Wing: Webby saddle hackle, 1 or 2 wraps

Photo by McTage Tanner.

Cohen's Shaggin' Dragon—Pat Cohen

Hook: Gamakatsu L10-2H, size 6

Eyes: Medium Black bead chain

Thread: Danvilles Flat Waxed Nylon 210, Hot Orange

Flashback Olive Brown

Rib: Ultra Wire, Hot Yellow, medium

Body: Olive Laser Dub

Legs: Olive Wiggle Dub

Wing Case: Turkey Flat coated with CCG Hydro

Tail: Olive Mallard Flank Feather

Photo by McTage Tanner.

Jan's Draggin—Orvis

Hook: Long shank nymph hook, size 6

Thread: Olive

Eyes: Black bead chain

Body: Olive rabbit dubbing and peacock crystal chenille, wound together

Collar: Olive grizzly hen hackle

Head: Olive rabbit dubbing

Photo by Tuck Scott.

Adam Hope's Dragon—Adam Hope

Hook: Gamakatsu SL45, sizes 6-10
Thread: UNI-thread (6/0)
Collar: Schlappen hackle
Body: Brown craft foam, Bohemian yarn
Legs: Medium round rubber legs, brown
Eyes: Medium Mono Nymph Eyes

Photo by McTage Tanner.

Cohen's Flashback Damsel Nymph—Pat Cohen

Hook: Daiichi 1770, size 8
Thread: Danville Flat Waxed Nylon 210, Olive
Head: Dazzle Bead, Metallic Caddis Green, ⅛"
Tail: Olive Marabou
Body: Dark Shade Rainbow Scud Dub
Rib: Ultra Wire, Copper, size Brassie
Wing Case: Flashback Olive Brown
Legs: Ringneck Pheasant Rump Feather

Photo by McTage Tanner.

Living Damsel—Orvis

Hook: TMC 3769 nymph hook, size 10
Thread: 6/0 black thread
Tail: Braided Olive Marabou
Body: Forest Green Dubbing
Rib: Fine Gold Wire
Eyes: Black bead chain
Shell casing: Pheasant Tail
Wings: Olive pheasant rump

Photo by Tuck Scott.

Adam Hope's Damsel—Adam Hope

Hook: 3X long nymph hook, size 10
Thread: UNI-thread, 8/0 olive dun
Eyes: Medium Mono Nymph Eyes
Tail: Saddle Hackle, olive
Body: Hareline Dubbin, olive brown
Ribbing: Body Glass, olive or brown
Shellback: Scud-Back, dark olive
Legs: Mini Centipede Legs, brown

Photo by Tuck Scott.

Damsel Bugger—Mark Erdosy

Hook: Tiemco 5263 and 5262, sizes 6–14
Thread: Danville 70 Denier to match color of fly
Eyes: Light mono, medium black bead chain, or heavy lead dumbbell
Tail: Marabou
Body: Dubbing of your choice to match color of fly
Hackle: Schlappen secured with wire or Wapsi stretch tubing
Back: Thin Skin on both sides of fly

Photo by McTage Tanner.

Mr. P's Real Damsel—Jim Pankiewicz

Hook: Tiemco 2457 or 2487, size 12
Thread: Black or olive
Eyes: Nickel-colored brass, size 7/64
Tail: Trimmed rabbit fur, golden olive
Body: Dubbed rabbit fur, golden olive
Legs: Hungarian partridge

Photo by McTage Tanner.

Dry Flies

Traditional dry fly patterns can be very effective carp patterns.

Photo by Dan Frasier.

EVERY TIME I TELL SOMEONE that their dry fly box is an essential item for any carp outing, I am met with the same responses.

"You can catch them on dries?"

"I thought they were bottom feeders."

"Are you sure they do that here?"

For the record, the answers are yes, sometimes, and probably..

It really is a strange path when you think about it. Fly fishing hit its stride in America with the popularization of the Catskills dry fly over traditional wet fly. To this day, dry fly fishing essentially defines the sport to most nonanglers, who imagine Brad Pitt shadow casting over a bawling river. For a couple hundred years the sport has essentially spread out from the dry fly in concentric circles until eventually you are throwing articulated streamers to musky or completely synthetic flies to tarpon. That is to say where we can get them on dries we do; where we can't, we have adapted.

Carp, as they have with everything else, turned that paradigm on its head. Rather than asking, "Can we get them on dries, and if so, how?" and then working our way out, carp fly fishermen approached carp as if it were a redfish, asking, "Can we get them tailing and eating crustaceans, and if so, how?" From there we have worked our way out in waves, learning new flies and techniques to accommodate the other situations we might encounter. One of those waves has led us back to the dry fly. It's proven to be a more than feasible method to take a carp; it may even be the most universally effective way. Strange, since top water dominates anywhere else, that we didn't start there for carp.

Regardless of how we got here, the dry fly is quickly finding it's way into the chest packs of most serious carp fly fishermen. It's not that they head to the water expecting to find rising carp. It's that you may find carp eating on the surface at any time on most waters in

North America, and if you don't have dry flies with you, you are out of luck. When you do stumble upon a pod of rising carp and you are ready with the right flies, you've found something special. There isn't another fish I know of that offers the chance to catch a twenty-or even thirty-pound fish on a dry fly. And I do mean chance. So many things can go wrong that hooking and landing the biggest of carp on the tiny hooks needed to float a fly is very difficult.

First off, the fish are moderately selective. Now don't get me wrong, they aren't like some well-trained tailwater trout in their demands on a fly fisherman. However, they do need to see a fly that is a reasonable approximation of whatever they are eating. Where they really get picky is that they demand that a fly moves on the water like the real thing. For the most part, that means they need a perfect dead drift. This can get tricky. Carp usually rise in slack or even still water. You have to cast well in front of them because the water isn't broken in any way to mask the landing of your fly. That being said, the carp also isn't gong to help you out. It will only rarely move for a fly. So you are stuck needing to lead the fish by a mile, get a dead drift in a slack current, and hope that the end of that drift is directly at the fish you are targeting. There's a lot going on here.

Once you do put that perfect drift on your huge fish, you have a second problem. The carp just aren't very good at eating things off the surface. Their mouths aren't built for it, and their eyes are in the wrong places on their heads, so they miss flies more frequently than I would prefer. Man, if only I got to make up the rules. When they don't miss the fly on their own, their mouths and the casual way they eat dry flies also hurt your chances of getting a clean eat. Carp don't come up

Photo by Targhee Boss.

from under a fly to eat it. Instead they will have half of their mouth already sticking out of the water as they skim mouth along the top looking for food. That leaves them with almost no suction power for moving the fly into their skim. Your fly has to practically fall into their open lips without being pushed away by the lips hitting your tippet or pulled away by your leader not having enough slack.

If you try this enough, you will get the right drift and an eat, and then you have another problem. You now have a fish weighing five times as much as the biggest trout you've ever caught hooked on a thin wire hook. And that fish is not happy. Hooked carp will frequently jump when you first stick them with a dry fly since they are facing up already. After that, they run harder than any other freshwater fish. Their ability to process oxygen efficiently means they don't tire quickly and can recover with ease if you let them sit on the bottom and sulk, assuming the fish didn't head for the weeds.

Fortunately, it isn't all bad news. Carp will often afford you several shots at the same fish with the dry fly. For some reason, carp that are

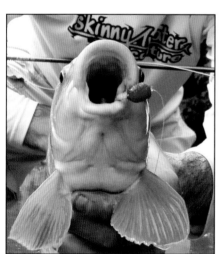

Photo by Tim Creasy.

spooked will return to surface to feed more quickly than they do in other feeding situations. They also feed in large pods, so you can get multiple shots at multiple fish for an extended period of time.

Determining when the carp will be on the surface is difficult. Unless you have pegged a specific mulberry bush that you know they will feed under or you saw them working a backwater the day before, it will be difficult to know when you'll see carp feeding on top. You won't find them sipping midges or eating grasshoppers every time you go out, but you could find them doing it at any time. So have your dry fly box ready, and when you get a chance to fish to rising carp, take it. It might be your most productive carp fly fishing day of the year.

6
Dries

THE MORE PEOPLE I TALK TO ABOUT CARP FLY FISHING the more important I think dry flies will become in the pursuit of carp. For now, this is a relatively unexplored area of what is a young pursuit. Clooping is the unofficial onomatopoeic term used to describe carp when eating on the surface.

On my home water, dry flies may be the most important flies I carry. In the spring, carp here spend a significant amount of time feeding on surface midges. Throughout the summer, they can be found in backwaters or along banks and scum lines sucking in anything from plant matter to caddis flies. Occasionally, a good breeze will blow a bunch of cottonwood seeds into that water, and the carp line up to have at the buffet. By late fall, hoppers have become a real part of the carp's diet, and eventually the smaller autumn flies will again bring them to the surface. In some ways it reminds me of trout fishing. When there is enough food on the top, the carp will rise to it. If there isn't, they will remain subsurface; it takes more stuff on top to entice the carp because a big trout may be twenty inches while a big carp is twenty pounds.

DESCRIPTION

A vast majority of the dry flies used for carp are simply traditional patterns. In the pursuit of the very picky trout, tiers have already done a remarkable job imitating most bugs that we find on the surface. Carp are not as picky as trout about pattern, color, or size within reason. Add to that the fact that carp will have seen few, if any, flies over the course of their lives, and pattern isn't all that important for most hatches. However, there are a few hatches that are especially important in carp fly fishing. Obviously, new patterns for those flies needed to be developed, and some creative solutions are already floating around. Pun absolutely intended.

Mulberries are one of the storied hatches in carp fly fishing. These berries grow along the edges of streams or rivers and plop into the water when they are ripe. Carp simply love them. These small fruits, about

Carp find a cottonwood seed nearly irresistible.

Photo by McTage Tanner

an inch across, tend to be white as they mature, deepening into a red and eventually a dark purple as they become ripe. They look something like a raspberry in that they are lumpy and slightly oblong.

Another hatch specific to carp fishing is the cottonwood seed. The fast-growing cottonwood tree requires a significant amount of water and is naturally found around rivers and lakes. In the spring, the female trees form pods that burst open with individual cotton-like seeds. These seeds are then blown into the water where they float until they find a wet and silty bank to come to rest. This ensures there is plenty of wet soil available for the seed to germinate. All of this adds up to blizzards of white fluff floating on the water after a good spring breeze. The carp go nuts for it.

PATTERN CHARACTERISTICS

Match . . . the . . . hatch. That's about all there is to it. The characteristics of traditional dry fly patterns are pretty well known. As for the mulberry and cottonwood seed flies, there are a couple of things a tier should keep in mind. Mulberries make a distinctive plops when they hit the water and ride a little low as they drift. These flies, while still floating, should be tied with enough material to imitate the plop and the sunken drift.

Cottonwood seeds, on the other hand, float down to the surface. They ride relatively flat as they drift in the current, and the seed is a distinctive brown spot in the otherwise white fly. All of this may or may not make much of a difference, but it is sure nice when your fly looks just like the real thing.

PRESENTATION

All dry flies for carp should be presented with a dead drift. Even carp that are eating grasshoppers are either unable or unwilling to eat a fly that is moving very much. Instead they seem to prefer the fly bobbing helplessly in their feeding path.

Things are a little tricky when still water fishing for carp with a dry fly. Carp are remarkably bad at eating off of the surface. Their mouths are set low on their head for bottom feeding, and when eating at the surface, only the top half of their mouth protrudes above the water. That means that they have lost all of their suction power. They simply mouth their way across the surface letting the fly drift in. Don't get me wrong,

Mulberry flies are larger and denser than traditional dry flies to emulate the sound of a berry falling in the water.
Photo by Adam Hope.

the carp will move to a dry when they are trying to eat that particular item, they just can't pull the fly toward them with suction. The effect is that you should try to present the fly to a carp in the line it is moving as it feeds along the surface. Leave a little slack in the leader or tippet so the fly is offering no resistance to being pulled into the carp's mouth. If you find that the carp are trying to eat your fly and can't, it's probably because your tippet won't allow the fly to fall back into the carp's mouth. This is also why a dropper setup is particularly ineffective in still water. When the carp attempts to eat the dry, the tippet hanging down will hit the fish's lower lip and actually move the dry fly forward away from the fish.

Fly floatant is a wonderful invention and is sometimes required to keep a fly on top. That said, carp have such a well-developed sense of taste that it can alert them to the fact that something is not right with your fly. If you are fishing in still water and the carp are only moving to your fly slowly, try to go without floatant whenever possible. This will reduce the likelihood that the taste or smell of the floatant on the water is alerting the fish that something is wrong.

FLY PATTERN

Catch's Seed—Eric Beebe

Hook. Gaper, size 8
Thread: White 6/0 UNI-thread
Body: Rainbow Sow Scud
    Dubbing
Wing: Stacked Deer Hair Pushed
    flat
Top of Wing: 2 mm foam super
    glued in the middle

Photo by McTage Tanner.

Carp Cottonwood Seed— Brad Befus

Hook: Caddis Pupa Tiemco
    TMC 2487 #12-14
Thread: White
Wing: 4-6 white CDC Fibers

Photo by McTage Tanner.

Anderson's Cotton Fly— Geoff Anderson

Hook: Allen Fly Fishing N203
    #10–14
Underbody: White thread
Body: White foam
Tuff or Wing: Marabou fluff
    from the bottom of a white
    schlappen feather

Photo by McTage Tanner.

Hammond's CDC Seed

Hook: Scud hook, size 14
Thread: Flat, white rayon
Body: Thread wraps
Hackle: White CDC wrapped around a
  foam post
Post: Brown micro foam

Photo by Tuck Scott.

Elkwing Caddis—Orvis

Hook: Dry fly, size 10-18
Thread: 6/0 or 3/0 Uni
Body: Fine fur or synthetic dubbing
Rib: Fine gold wire
Wing: Elk or deer hair
Hackle: Brown from neck cape

Photo by McTage Tanner.

Parachute Adam's—Orvis

Hook: Dry fly, size 10–20
Thread: 3/0–8/0, color to match fly
Tail: Hackle fibers, Microfibbets, Deer,
  Elk, or Moose hair
Wing: Calf Tail, Elk, or Deer hair,
  Hackle Tips

Photo by McTage Tanner.

Abdomen: Dubbing, color to match
  fly
Hackle: Saddle or Neck, color to match fly

Stimulator—Orvis

Hook: Dry fly, size 6–16
Thread: Red UTC 140 Denier
Tail: Deer or Elk hair tips
Rib: Copper wire
Body: Yellow dry-fly dubbing
Body hackle: Brown dry-fly saddle
Wing: Deer or Elk hair
Head hackle: Grizzly dry-fly saddle
Head: Hot Orange Ice Dubbing

Photo by Tuck Scott.

Schroader's Parachute Hopper—Orvis

Hook: 2x long dry fly, size 8–14
Thread: Cream 6/0
Body: Yellow or Olive dubbing
Wing: Mottled Turkey quill
Hackle: Grizzly, parachute style
Legs: Knotted Pheasant Tail
Wing Post: White Calf Tail

Photo by Tuck Scott.

Orr's Sinking Dingleberry— Austin Orr

Hook: Gamakatsu Octopus Circle size 8 or Daiichi 3111 size 2
Thread: Danville 3/0, chartreuse
Body: Chenille yarn in black or dark purple, tied in and then loosely palmered forward before over-wrapping with thread

Photo by McTage Tanner.

Orr's Floating Dingleberry—Austin Orr

Photo by McTage Tanner.

Hook: Gamakatsu Octopus Circle size 8 or Daiichi 3111 size 2
Thread: Danville 3/0, chartreuse
Body: Black closed cell foam cut to taper at each end with thickest part in the middle

Anderson's Berry Go Plop—Geoff Anderson

Photo by McTage Tanner.

Hook: #4 Gamakatsu octopus hook
Tail: Green rubber leg or clump of green goose wing
Underfoam: 2 mm foam
Body: Ice UV Dub, black, peacock, dun, rust
Eyes: Black bead chain, optional

Plopper Mullberry—Mike Schultz

Photo by McTage Tanner.

Hook: Daiichi 1120, size 6
Stem: Round rubber leg, green
Body: Spun deer body hair, purple and trimmed to shape
Post: Rainy's White float foam…small

Dropper Mullberry—Mike Schultz

Hook: Daiichi 1120, size 6
Stem: Round rubber leg, green
Body: Purple Mcfly foam, trimmed

Photo by McTage Tanner.

Super Meat

The exciting sight of large carp moving through clear, shallow water allows the angler to observe behavior and devise a strategy.

Photo by John "Montana" Bartlett.

IMAGINE FOR A MOMENT: The water is clear and deep. The bottom and surrounding landscape is defined by rock and sand. Very little in the way of vegetation exists to establish a layer upon which an ecosystem can form. The scene looks dead and sterile. When you see the dark shapes in the water for the first time, you have trouble convincing yourself they aren't just more rocks. Waves and light can make even stationary objects appear to swim. Slowly your mind wraps itself around what you are seeing. It's a dozen or so fish cruising along with purpose. They may average fifteen pounds with the real bosses running into the thirties. One hundred eighty pounds of fish moving together like a pack of wolves hunting anything that moves. So this is what they were talking about.

Carp present a breathtakingly unique situation when they are found in sterile or deep water environments—unique to carp fishing and, in fact, unique to freshwater fishing as a whole. They become hunters looking for larger prey items and willing to chase them down to eat them. That itself is unusual for carp. In most situations, carp prefer to forage rather than hunt—it is what they are built for. However, when sufficient forage items just aren't available, they will do what they do best: adapt.

What makes this situation unique to all freshwater is that the carp don't stop being a shoaling fish. Most freshwater hunters are solitary. They will find strong ambush points, hide, and then chase down unwary food items that come too close. This is how pike, musky, bass, and others feed. While you can still find these fish in larger numbers, you don't find them in a shoal—just a bunch of individual fish that happen to be in one place. Carp, on the other hand, still prefer to live in large groups and move together. They don't sit in ambush points and wait for prey. When carp become hunters, they are more like wolves than cheetahs. They move in a pack and keep on the move: cruising, peeling off to eat a spooked prey item, and rejoining, always cruising.

There are a few well-known destinations where the carp hunt large prey items. The Great Lakes are probably the most famous locations. The scale of the Great Lakes as flats fisheries is difficult to imagine, but this may help put it in perspective. There are more than 10,000 miles of shoreline along the Great Lakes. That's about four trips from New York to Los Angeles. Not every one of those miles holds bands of marauding carp, but many of them do. There is still a long way to go in the exploration of these massive bodies of water as potential carp

Carp move in groups when hunting large prey.
Photo by John "Montana" Bartlett.

In certain locations, catching carp requires very large flies.
Photo by Cam Mortenson.

fisheries, and as more and more people go looking, they discover ever more shallow bays and large flats. When water temperature is right, any one of these bays could hold great shoals of large carp. All along the Great Lakes, there are shallow bays and flats where at the right time of year, the carp will come and feed on gobies and other baitfish that live in the rocks. Fly fishermen from around the United States are making the trek to experience this awesome opportunity, but the Great

Photo by Targhee Boss.

Lakes aren't the only places carp exhibit such predatory behavior.

Many large sterile reservoirs hold fish that are primarily cruisers and hunters. The Blackfoot reservoir is one of these well-known destinations. This large manmade lake is full of a genetic variation of carp called Mirror Carp. The genetic mutation is relatively rare and leaves the fish with large scaleless areas on the body. The rarity of finding these fish in the wild make them highly sought-after fly fishing

targets. On the Blackfoot, these carp have adapted to the environment in a way that makes the fishery even more special: They have become predators. As we will see, the flies used to catch Blackfoot Mirror Carp are large and juicy. Long casts and strips are the order of the day as these large rare fish will hunt down the fly and attack it. It's a special place.

Scattered around the United States are other large sterile bodies of water that hold carp that will take big flies. Deep reservoirs and large dams are a good place to start looking. The reservoir, if rocky and lifeless enough, can hold predatory carp. The deepest end, as near to the dam as possible, is the most promising. Additionally, near the dams of large tailwaters can be deep and sterile, and the carp that

Sterile water bodies can produce predatory carp that require large flies.

Photo by John "Montana" Bartlett.

live there are oftentimes quite willing to chase a fly when presented appropriately.

Places like this don't exist everywhere. For the most part, you will be fishing rivers and lakes where the carp are relatively passive eaters. However, even fish that spend most of their time foraging can become aggressive at certain times of year. During the spawn, carp that are taking a break from the rigors of spawning will lay along the outside edge of the spawning area. These fish can sometimes be induced to chase a large stripped fly. During baitfish season, when large amounts of small baitfish are around, carp sometimes begin to key on them as a food item. It all comes down to availability. If large prey is readily available and in concentrations heavy enough to be the primary food source for the carp, they will feed on it.

7
Great Lakes

The carp flats of the Great Lakes could be mistaken for bonefish flats in the Florida Keys.
Photo by Cam Mortenson.

THE MOST FAMOUS CARP FLATS IN THE UNITED STATES surround Beaver Island, Michigan. These islands, along with Grand Traverse Bay just across the water, are host to professional carp fly fishing guides and countless destination anglers every year. Kirk Deeter described these flats, with apologies to his friends fishing the saltwater flats all along the United States coasts, as "the best flats fishing in North America."

While these are the most famous flats on the Great Lakes, they may not be the most productive. People have begun to explore the bays and flats of all five of the Great Lakes and are catching fish on all of them. The truth is, we don't yet know where the best carp flat on the Great Lakes is because that flat may not yet be discovered.

All of this exploration has taught us a few things. Water temperature is the most critical factor determining whether the carp will be present on a given flat or not. The carp enter the bays to feed when the water temperature is higher in the bay than in the surrounding deeper water. An angler trying to find carp in the shallow flats of one of these massive bodies of water needs to pay attention to which direction the wind is blowing and how that moves the water into the bay. If a wind is blowing into the bay, it will push the water on the surface, warmed by the sun, into the bay and the cold water out. When you can find a flat or bay where the water is significantly warmer than the surrounding lake, the carp will show up. This seems to be a constant consideration no matter what bay on which lake you are searching.

Nearly all of the Great Lakes Super Meat flies originated in the Beaver Island area. Another interesting phenomenon, given the carp's traditional specialization in food by location, is that the same flies seem to be productive on a majority of the Great Lakes carp.

The Great Lakes offer fly anglers shots at fish in excess of 30 pounds.
Photo by Miles Christmas.

Great Lakes carp require long casts and a stripped fly.
Photo by John "Montana" Bartlett.

DESCRIPTION

Identifying the food item the carp are eating is as critical on Lake Michigan as it is in an urban pond. Luckily, the predominant food item has already been identified. Crayfish do exist throughout the Great Lakes and work well in larger sizes, but the most abundant prey on the Great Lakes is the Round Goby, an invasive species that was introduced into the Great Lakes through ballast water in the 1990s. This small fish is a voracious predator with a penchant for the also invasive zebra mussel. Just to be clear, the introduced carp are feeding on the invasive goby, which in turn eats the invasive Zebra Mussel—a food chain of aliens. gobies spend the daytime hours hidden amongst the rocks and venture out at night to feed. They are a small, soft-bodied fish with a fused pectoral fin that works like a suction cup on rocks. They can range in size up to ten inches in length but are frequently found much smaller than that. In many ways, they look and act like the native sculpin and have been known to outcompete them once introduced to a body of water.

Carp on the Great Lakes have added gobies to their preferred list of food items. Shoals of carp will cruise the rocky flats, and when a small goby is flushed, a member of the shoal will peel off and chase it down as it dives for a hiding place in the rocks. The carp of the Great Lakes have become quite adept at feeding on these little baitfish and will use their unique mouths and suction to pull gobies out of hiding places.

PATTERN CHARACTERISTICS

While many different patterns are effective, depending on the situation and preferences of the fish, there are a few things that most of them seem to have in common. Rabbit strip is probably the most common tying material seen in all of these patterns. It's lifelike action in the water and ability to breathe and move even while sitting still has made it a favorite for most of these patterns.

Most freshwater streamers are tied for the purpose of drawing attention to themselves. They are the class clowns of flies. More aggressive fish, such as bass and pike, seem to be willing to strike these flies, possibly out of aggression as much as to eat them. Carp streamers work a little differently. Muted colors are common with olives, browns, and tans being the most popular. Additions, such as flash or a bunch of rubber legs, and bright colors, such as whites or chartreuse, are rare because they will often scare fish. For the most part, the idea is still to emulate a food source, rather than draw attention. You are trying to present the carp with something that they think is whatever they are accustomed to eating. In nature, most prey items are built more to disguise than call attention to themselves, and your flies should reflect that.

The last common trait of these flies is that they are still weighted. Sometimes the rabbit strip itself will provide sufficient weight, but for the most part, bead chain or dumbbell eyes and often some wire will be necessary to get the flies down. The carp are still hunting for food on or near the bottom, and you will want your fly to act accordingly.

PRESENTATION

Just like all other carp, it is the fish's behavior that lets you know if they are a good target. Great Lakes carp that are players could be described as aggressive shoppers. Earlier we defined fish as shoppers if they are slowly and erratically cruising the bottom. Sometimes these fish will lunge or dip as they take something into their mouths. Great Lakes carp are really no different, only a little faster. Singles or small groups of fish showing this behavior will be your best targets. They may be cruising faster than they do on other waters, but they are still shopping. Large groups of

Photo by Travis Hammond.

fish that are going somewhere quickly are less likely to take a fly, and you risk spooking the entire flat.

Strips—that about sums it up. These flies are cast where you think they will get in front of a fish and stripped. So the presentation goes something like this. Cast beyond the path the fish is taking, being sure to lead them enough that the splash won't spook them. Strip the fly so it intersects the fish's path just ahead of them, and set the hook when the carp gets on the fly. Simple but not easy.

The stripping, in fact, becomes the variable that can be the difference between a great day and a bust. In some instances, the flies will need to be stripped quickly to look like a fleeing, fully healthy baitfish. Other times, a slow swim like a large leech working its way through the water will be most effective. I particularly enjoy giving my fly a twitch and a sink like a dying baitfish or even crawling it slowly along the bottom. The point is, there is no hard and fast presentation in this case. You have to decide how the food items are acting and manipulate your fly accordingly.

FLY PATTERNS

Martinez's Goby—Steve Martinez

Photo by McTage Tanner.

Hook: Umpqua, TMC 200R, size 4-6

Eyes: Medium dumbbell in red

Tail: Rag yarn

Tail: 2-4 strands of copper tinsel

Body: Olive brown Ice Dub with a natural guinea palmered through it

First Collar: Hareline Dubbin, Hare's Ice Dub in peacock

Second Collar: Rag yarn

Head: Deer body hair, brown or olive

Morlock's Goby—Kevin Morlock

Head Section

Photo by McTage Tanner.

Hook: Tiemco, TMC 105, size 4

Eye: Wapsi Dumbbell Eyes in yellow, size medium

Note: Secure the eyes in the middle of the hook, cement, and put aside to dry

Tail Section

Hook: Any light and cheap short shank hook—it gets cut off at the bend

Tail: Medium-Small pheasant feather with lots of contrast

Hackles: Build forward starting with small then progressively larger pheasant feathers—the tail section should take between 4-5 feathers to complete

Note: Choose contrasting feather colors to give the fly a mottled look

Joining tail section with the middle section and building the middle section:

Cut: Cut the tail hook off at the bend

Join: 6 inches of 20# Power Pro or another braided casting line

Hook: Any light and cheap short shank hook—it gets cut off at the bend

Hackles: Build forward starting with medium then progressively larger pheasant feathers—this section will only take 2-3 feathers as they are now larger

Joining middle and tail with the head section and finishing the head:

Cut: Cut the tail hook off at the bend

Joint: 6 inches of 20# Power Pro or another braided casting line

Hackle(s): 1 or 2 large pheasant feathers

Throat: Pinch of yellow Marabou

Collar and head behind the eyes: Spun deer body hair

Front head and between the eyes: Deer body hair applied with a dubbing loop

Martinez's Depth Charge—Steve Martinez

Hook: TMC 200R, size 4-6

Eyes: Large yellow-red lead eyes

Body Weight: 12 or so wraps of lead wire

Tail: Black barred brown Marabou

Body: Olive brown UV Polar chenille

First Collar: Yellow mallard

Second Collar: Red Ice Dub

Head: Peacock colored Cactus Dubbing, brushed rearward

Photo by Tuck Scott.

Morlock's Beast Bait—Kevin Morlock

Hook: Daiichi 1530, size 4
Eyes: Large red lead eyes
Tail or Body: Barred yellow bunny strip
Hackle: Olive Schlappen
Head: Root beer Estaz

Photo by McTage Tanner.

Frankenstein Sculpin—Steve Martinez

Hook: Daiichi 2161, size 2
Tail: Barred olive Marabou
Body: Olive brown Ice Dub with yellow mallard flank palmered through
Collar: Black lazer dub
Back: Olive mallard flank
Peck Fins: Barred olive Marabou tied in half body length
Olive Sculpin Helmet: Size small

Photo by McTage Tanner.

Morlock's Bunny Craw— Kevin Morlock

Hook: Daiichi 2151, size 1
Weight: Lead wire, 12 or so wraps of .030"
Tail Claws: Bunny strip tied so that they spread
Claw Flash: 2 strands of blue and 2 strands of red Hareline Dubbin Krystal Flash
Tail Color Accent: Small pinch of yellow Marabou
Tail Hackle: Schlappen
Eyes: Large bead chain, lead eyes, or whatever your conditions call for
Inner Body: Yarn that matches the Polar Chenille, tapered toward tail
Outer Body: Hareline Dubbin, Polar Chenille

Photo by McTage Tanner.

Hammerhead Rough Dub— Christopher Vargo

Photo by Tuck Scott.

Hook: Dai Riki #930, sizes 2–6

Fore Eye: Lead eye or medium size 6, large size 4, or extra large size 2 bead chain

Mid eye: Length of four beads from corresponding medium, large, or extra large bead chain

Claws: Two clumps of squirrel tail, not stacked, positioned and post wrapped at least once

Body: Medium, long, or extra long dubbing mixed 50/50 with ⅝"-¾" cut squirrel tail, synthetic yak also works as an additive

Morlock's Rock Hopper—Kevin Morlock

Photo by McTage Tanner.

Hook: Daiichi 2151, size 2

Tail One: Finn raccoon zonker in tan

Tail Two: Flashabou Accent, grizzly, in black or copper

Body: Senyo's Laser Dub in hot pink

Rib: Medium copper wire

Underwing: Wapsi Palmer Chenille in medium, root beer, a couple wraps

Hackle: Brown Schlappen

Outerwing: Flashabou Accent, grizzly in black or copper

Underhead: Any yarn to build a perfect fit for the Sculpin Helmet

Head: Fish Skull, Sculpin Helmet in brown, small

Morlock's Tailer Teaser— Kevin Morlock

Hook: Daiichi 1710, size 4

Photo by McTage Tanner.

Lead: 25 wraps of .025" lead wire
Eyes: Red, size small
Tail: Enrico Puglisi 3D fibers in everglades
Tail Flash: Orange crystal flash
Body: Root beer Estaz
Rubber Legs: Brown and black barred
Head: Orange Estaz

Midnight Meat Train—Jean Paul Lipton

Photo by McTage Tanner.

Hook: Gamakatsu B10S Stinger, size 2
Thread: UNI-thread 6/0, Fire Orange
Tail: Magnum Zonker, Black
Legs: Hareline Loco Legs, Green Turtle Grass, Grizzly Flutter Legs, Chartreuse Barred Black
Body: Pseudo Hackle 1.5", black or Magnum Zonker, black, not cross cut
Thorax: Roughfisher's custom spectral seal sub dubbing, peacock
Eyes: Painted Lead Eyes (1/20 oz), large, Gold

8
Baitfish

CARP HAVE ADAPTED TO PRIMARILY EAT BAITFISH IN places other than the Great Lakes and will chase flies with abandon year-round. If you get an opportunity to fish locations like this, count your blessings and tie on a baitfish pattern.

Most carp forage on small, easy-to-catch animals. They live off the nymphs, crayfish, and worms that can be had without expending much energy. Things get interesting when these small prey items aren't readily available. For most species of fish, the absence of primary food sources translates to the absence of those fish but not so for carp. Carp are amazingly adaptive to new environments, and on some sterile reservoirs and tailwaters where there isn't enough food on the bottom, the carp are left looking for another food source. In many cases, they've turned to baitfish.

There are a few telltale signals that carp are eating other fish. First of all, be sure that the body of water meets the criteria needed to create meat-eating carp. The lake or river should be relatively devoid of small life forms, usually with rocky or hard bottoms. Given the choice, carp will always choose the easiest meal. If the bottom isn't hard, it should be at least pretty barren. Be careful in your assessment here. The Columbia River is one of the storied carp waters in the United States. At first blush, the clear water and rocky gravel bottoms seem like a quintessential baitfish fishery. If you dig a little deeper (literally) you'll find that buried in that gravel are millions of mussels. That's all the carp will eat on the Columbia. So we go

The highly-regarded mirror carp of the Blackfoot Reservoir will only eat large baitfish patterns.
Photo by Brent Wilson.

back to the most important rule in fly fishing for carp. Know your forage.

Very deep water, such as at the base of large dams, is another habitat. Many reservoirs will have one end with extremely steep riprap shorelines that become deep quickly. This end of the reservoir is near the dam and can be a great place to find carp feeding on baitfish. The water here is not conducive to plant growth on the bottom, which is a requirement for a strong base forage layer to the food chain. Carp found here might very well be accustomed to working harder for their food, and a juicy meal like a baitfish can often entice them.

The other side of the dam, the tailwater, is also a good place to look for baitfish-eating carp. If you can get close enough to the dam, the banks are usually steep and rocky, and the water is deep and pretty sterile. This water is moving quickly and is too deep for light to get to the bottom to induce plant growth. Carp here will probably be hunters.

These are bodies of water where carp specialize in eating baitfish most of the time. However, that isn't the only way to get a carp to eat a baitfish fly. As discussed at the beginning of the book, carp not only adapt to the environment they are in, they adjust their preferred food source throughout the course of the season based on the availability of forage at that time and in that body of water. Sometimes, small baitfish are the most plentiful source of calories in all bodies of water, including in more traditional carp fisheries, such as ponds, lakes, and rivers. Here, small baitfish can make up a portion of a carp's diet at certain times of year or under the right conditions. Although carp feeding on baitfish in these richer environments is a spotty phenomenon at best, it is too important not to mention.

Carp are both opportunistic in their feeding habits and selective with regard to the food organisms that they will be eating at any particular time or place. When you combine those two ideas, you are left with a fish that could be eating anything but is most likely eating only one thing. This rule holds true with small baitfish. When they are plentiful and easy, carp can hone in on them for a period of time, and you have to be prepared to take advantage of that fact. I've heard anglers refer to baitfish season, which seems to vary from water to water. Basically, whenever the baby fish are hatching most plentifully on your water, carp may be keying on them.

DESCRIPTION

I'm going to assume you know what a baitfish looks like. It's a tiny fish. What you may not know is what carp look like when they are feeding on baitfish. Luckily, there are some distinct behaviors that can tip off the angler that the carp in your area are in the mood for sushi.

When carp become hunters in sterile environments, they act differently than they do anywhere else. They are gathering food in a unique way, and that creates a set of behaviors only displayed on these bodies of water. Once you've established that the water you are on fits the correct criteria for baitfish hunting carp, you should then look at the behavior of the fish. When you can match the right environment with the appropriate behavior, you can be pretty certain what the fish are eating and which fish are good targets.

Carp that are hunting are moving. We like to call these cruising carp, and they are good targets on baitfish water and bad targets elsewhere. This is how an angler could discern that the Columbia River carp aren't eating baitfish. Everywhere they are tailing, and the cruisers won't take a fly. If you can see carp tailing, there is something on the bottom they are feeding on, which means they aren't looking for baitfish. In deep water places, such as tailwaters right at the dam or on the deep end of reservoirs, the carp will be high enough in the water column for you to see them. That means a long way from the bottom. Fish moving here have little reason to do so unless they are fleeing or hunting. When it looks like the fish are circulating in groups in this mid-column area, there is a good chance they are looking for food.

In richer bodies of water, the behavior carp show while eating baitfish is usually quite different than on sterile bodies of water. Remember, here the carp aren't eating baitfish because there isn't anything else. Here they are eating them because the baitfish are easier or more plentiful than traditional food items. If the carp were required to work as hard here to get baitfish as they are where there isn't a choice, they would simply eat something else.

At the most basic level, carp are masters of getting food without expending much energy. They don't fight currents, charge around after difficult-to-catch items, or try to hunt in open water. Carp prefer to have their food delivered rather than go pick it up themselves. These preferences don't change simply because baitfish are on the menu that day. The carp will find places to hold where the baitfish are delivered to them and relatively easy to catch; if you see carp stacked up at the bottom of a spillway or behind a hard riffle or waterfall, it's possible they are there to pick up stunned or injured baitfish. The same goes for rocky shorelines when wind and wave action may be buffeting the tiny fish against the shore. There is no guarantee that fish holding in these spots are eating baitfish. They could be eating anything that is prevalent, so it has to be the time of year when large numbers of small fish are around.

Another sign that carp are eating baitfish is to see them crashing the shoreline or the surface like stripers. This behavior is rare, but I've seen it happen. In situations such as these, a single carp or a shoal of them

Carp stack up under waterfalls and spillways to eat stunned or wounded baitfish.
Photo by Mike Frasier.

will use either the surface or the bank to hem in a school of small fish. The carp then charge into the school to stun the small fish and eat them. Don't confuse this with a solitary fish jumping and splashing. You'll know the difference when you see it.

I'd be remiss if I didn't mention fishing baitfish patterns during the spawn. Spawning fish can be maddeningly difficult to catch. They are right there in front of you splashing in the shallows, and they just aren't interested in taking your fly. That said, larger streamer patterns have been known to work when cast to fish that are lying just outside of the fray and resting from the rigors of the spawn. These flies, cast and bounced quickly along the bottom, can induce a charge and strike from carp that are either very hungry or are protecting the eggs. It's hard to know which. Because carp are broadcast spawners, there are no redds or nests, so it is generally believed that they don't defend the eggs from intrusive smaller fish. But when a twenty-five-pound fish crashes through seven inches of water to crush your fly, it's hard to shake the feeling that the carp was mad.

PATTERN CHARACTERISTICS

Outside of the Great Lakes, there hasn't been a ton of innovation in carp-specific baitfish patterns. There just isn't enough water that requires specialty flies to create a need to invent them. As more people take up the pursuit of carp with the fly rod, they will likely discover more water with baitfish-eating carp and develop new patterns. In the meantime, modifications to traditional baitfish patterns seem to do the trick. There are, however, certain characteristics that produce more carp than others. The first theme among carp streamers is that they tend to be on a small side, between 1–2½ inches. The carp don't seem to take flies larger than that as readily. Much smaller than that and the fly seems to not get noticed. Just as crucial as size is the action in the water. Baitfish flies for carp employ very soft, supple materials to create movement. Even while fishing the most aggressive carp, the angler will normally be stripping fairly slowly. That means you won't be creating much movement in the fly, so the fly should wiggle on its own. Materials such as marabou and rabbit strip breathe well underwater and give even still flies some lifelike motion. Bucktail and synthetics are used far more sparingly. The stiffness of these two materials works against carp anglers. Unless you are using bucktail simply to build the profile and then add more supple materials for movement, I would think twice about using much in my carp flies.

The third theme in carp streamers is color. Drab, dull, and natural are the order of the day. Olives, blacks, and grays all work, while chartreuse, yellows, and reds are rarely included. For the same reasons, flash and rubber legs are used only sparingly and only when they are needed to create either a profile or coloration that looks like the real thing.

PRESENTATION

How you present the fly depends on whether you are casting to fish that are primarily baitfish eaters or to fish in a rich body of water that are eating opportunistically for a short time. Let's talk about presenting to the predators first.

Photo by Brent Wilson.

Carp in deep or sterile environments are attuned to hunting. As mentioned earlier, they will normally be on the move and oftentimes in deep water. Presenting flies to these fish is simple in theory and difficult in practice. The theory is to let the fish notice the fly in front of them and then strip it away slowly like something fleeing. You should wait until your cruising carp come into range and then lead the front fish by a considerable amount. Strip the fly until it is directly in the path of the fish you are targeting and then let is sink. As the carp approaches, begin to strip the fly away from the fish is small erratic strips. If all goes right, the carp will notice the moving fly, peel off from the group, and follow until it catches and eats the fly. This whole process can take longer than you would like, and it's important to keep your fly at the right place in the water column. For that reason, I prefer to use lightly weighted flies in situations such as these. They give me better control of the sink rate.

When you are fishing carp in richer environments where baitfish aren't always on the menu, the fish aren't as willing to chase a fly. Here they are eating baitfish not because they have to but because for some reason, it has gotten easier than eating anything else. That opportunistic attitude helps to define how to present your fly to these fish. The best presentation is one that gives the appearance of a wounded or recently killed fish. The carp will be holding at the base of a spillway or in a current following a rough stretch of water and picking off easily captured baitfish that are wounded, stunned, or disoriented. The proper presentation in situations like this is a dead drift with a light or unweighted fish pattern. When that isn't working, a slow swing of a fly with small erratic strips can do the trick. Either way, you will get more hook if you make it as easy as possible for the carp.

FLY PATTERNS

DSP Monkey—Will Rice

Hook: Umpqua 2457, size 8 or 10
Bead: Metz bright bead 4.8 or 4.0
Eyes: Medium bead chain
Legs: Metz silly leggs
Underwing: Hareline northern bucktail
Overwing: Metz Zonker rabbit strip

Photo by McTage Tanner.

Carp Bugger—Christopher Vargo

Hook: Dai Riki #930, size 6, or
    alternative
Thread: Danvile 210
Eyes: Large or extra large bead chain, or
    lead placed forward
Tail: Marabou
Tail optional: 2 strands of crystal flash
Body: Dubbing mix or chenille
Hackle: Saddle hackle tied off behind the
    eyes

Photo by Tuck Scott.

Missouri Bugger—Christopher Vargo

Hook: Dai Riki #930/sl45, size 4–6
Eyes: Extra large bead chain or lead eyes
Tail: Marabou
Body: Your favorite carp dubbing color

Photo by Tuck Scott.

Bottom Creeper—Bennett Muraski

Hook: Gamakatsu B10S, size 6
Thread: 6/0 Uni
Eyes: Painted lead
Body: Ice dub, pheasant tail color was
    used in shown patterns
Legs: Golden barred Sili Legs
Wing or Tail: ⅛" Zonker strip

Photo by Tuck Scott.

White Death—James Hughes

Hook: Gamakatsu SC15, size 4
Eyes: Presentation mini lead eyes tied on top of hook shank
Tail: White Ice Fur
Body: Thread wraps

Collar One: 2 wraps of white
  rabbit spun in dubbing loop
  behind eyes
Collar Two: 1 to two wraps of
  Natural Mallard flank behind
  eyes
Wing: White Ice fur

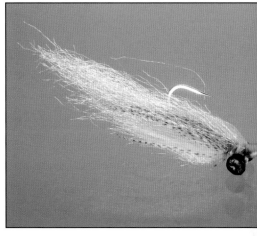

Photo by McTage Tanner.

Carp Muncher—Mike Schultz

Hook: Gamakatsu SL45, size 4-6
Eyes: Hareline Sunken dumbbell
  eyes, small
Tail: Ostrich Herl
Flash: A couple strands of red or
  copper flashabou mixed in with
  ostrich
Collar: White or olive grizzly soft
  hackle
Head: Rabbit spun in a dubbing
  loop

Photo by McTage Tanner.

Black Ops—Christoper Vargo

Hook: Dai Riki #930 or
  Gamakatsu sl 45 bonefish hook,
  size 6–8
Eyes: Large or extra large bead
  chain or lead eyes
Tail: Clump of turkey feathers to
  match body
Body: Black dubbing of your
  choice

Photo by Tuck Scott.

Wilson's Blackfoot Blood Leech—Brent Wilson

Hook: 3XL downeye streamer
  hook, size 8
Weight: Black bead head, 5/32"
Body: Black and burgundy
  simiseal dubbing
Tail: Black marabou tail

Photo by McTage Tanner.

PART

V

Universal

I KNOW I'VE BEATEN YOU OVER THE HEAD WITH THE idea that you have to know the forage of the carp you are casting to if you want to catch them. Carp are the most selective species of fish I've encountered, which is exactly what fly designers are working so hard to address. Stalking, presentation, detecting the take, and fighting the fish are hard enough without having the added insecurity of fly selection. So designers have set out to design flies that anglers can tie on with confidence regardless of forage.

The Holy Grail for any fly tier is to create that one pattern that every fish will eat. Over the years, tiers have created fantastic flies that can catch fish on most waters, such as the Adams and the Wooly Bugger. These are flies that stand a pretty good chance of producing regardless of the hatch, the location, or the water you are fishing. Carp fly designers are sitting in dank basements, drinking beer, and combining ingredients in unholy ways to create the one fly that will catch fish everywhere. For lack of a better term, we'll call this new genre universal flies.

Universal flies attempt to let carp see what they want to see in a fly pattern.

Photo by Elek Erdosy.

If you can't stop the carp from wanting to eat only what is in front of them, then your fly needs to look like whatever is in front of the carp. The trick to creating a universal fly, then, is to make it look a little like everything. That way, regardless of the forage, the carp may still mistake it for whatever its preferred forage item is at that moment.

Two distinct groups of flies have emerged from this thought process. The first are traditional egg and spawn flies. Egg and spawn flies are pretty specialized patterns in most forms of fly fishing. They work when fish are eating eggs, and then you put them away. When fly fishing for carp, they are used as a universal fly. They can address carp feeding on any amorphous white or pale-colored item. That might be the floating bodies

of dead clams, sunken terrestrial vegetation, maggots, or fish eggs themselves. An
egg fly could be mistaken for any number
of possible carp food items.

Frankenstein inspires the other approach
to finding a universal carp fly: Pick the best
parts of a few traditional patterns and tie
them all on the same hook. John "Montana" Bartlett's Hybrid pattern is a great
example. The underlying, or base, fly is an
olive soft hackle with a long hackle collar.
This fly alone could easily be a damselfly
nymph or any number of leggy underwater insects. The eyes and general profile of

Photo by Dan Frasier.

the fly could also be mistaken as a crayfish. When the red chenille
tail is added, the fly could be more things. It could be a clam with a
siphon sticking out or a worm burrowing under a rock. The imitation
depends on how you present and manipulate the fly rather than the
particular pattern. So when John hits the Columbia River with just
this fly tied on, he is effectively fishing a five-fly rig. One fly is presenting the carp with many different options. As John so eloquently puts it,
"They just look like food."

Even this most universal of subgroups has managed to splinter into
weighted flies versus unweighted flies. It is practically impossible to
get a carp to change the depth at which it is feeding; carp that are tailing will need a weighted fly to get down to them, while carp that are
feeding in the middle of the water column won't dive for a fly. Even
with a universal fly, it is still important to figure out your forage. For
one thing, it will let you know how the fly should be presented to the
fish. You'll know how far a fish is likely to move for a fly. And you'll
know whether to strip the line or fish it dead drift and whether you
should plop it on the carp's dinner plate or sneak it away from the
carp's path.

The other important thing the forage will tell you is which carp
you should target with your universal fly. If the carp are eating baitfish, you'll be looking for moving fish. If they are eating nymphs, it's

Targeting feeding fish with universal patterns is a good way increase your chances of hooking up.

Photo by Will Rice.

the fish that are grubbing around in the muck. The forage, as much as anything else, indicates which fish are the players and which are not. You'll still want to focus your efforts on the most actively feeding fish. They are the easiest to stalk and the most likely to mistake your monstrosity of a fly for food.

9
Eggs

ONE MAN FOREVER CHANGED MY VIEW OF CARP FLY fishing. His name is Gregg Martin, and he is the strongest proponent of the use of egg flies that I have ever met, but he doesn't preach eggs in the usual way. Gregg doesn't run a blog. He doesn't catch huge numbers or massive fish. What he does is he catches fish when, by all rights, he shouldn't.

In 1976 Gregg enlisted in the Army and served as a paratrooper stationed in Alaska until 1980. Despite the Korean War–era clothes and equipment and the Alaskan cold, Gregg loved it. Alaska was where Gregg wanted to be, and the US Army was making that happen for him. Following his service, Gregg became an Alaskan Smokejumper. Now he had found his calling. He would teach in the villages in the winter and fight fire in the summer, all in his beloved Alaska. Nothing but forced retirement at age 55 was going stop him. In 1985 Gregg was up a rope hanging parachutes to dry when he fell, leaving him paralyzed from the chest down.

Twenty-nine years after the accident, Gregg is still out there fly fishing. Where lesser men would have hung up the fly rod and lamented their misfortune, Gregg devised fly patterns and fishing techniques that allowed him to be successful on the water he could access. His specialized off-road wheelchair and pure determination get him places where he can get good access to water. Gregg often fishes alone, and has spent years devising methods that will take fish in these areas. For most, fishing means going to where the fish will respond to how we like to fish. For Gregg, it's about figuring out how to respond to what the fish want where he can get. Carp fishing, for most of us, is about stalking, climbing, and belly crawling. We scurry over rocks, push through brush, and cover many miles of water throughout the course of a season. We pass on fish that aren't showing the right body language. If the carp doesn't look like a viable feeding fish, we move on to the next one. For Gregg, none of this is a possibility. Gregg has to think in terms of available access. What water can he get to and how should it be fished? Effectively he's turned carp fishing on its head.

Even fish that are sunning rather than eating are good targets with an egg fly.

Photo by Will Rice.

Accepted dogma in fly fishing for carp is that you must find players and cast only to them. Find the most likely fish and catch it. If the fish in front of you aren't feeding or are too deep, you move on. Obviously, that's not an option in Gregg's case. So what do you do when the only place you can fish has carp that don't want to eat? You figure out how to make them want to eat. Gregg has made an art form of turning negative fish into players. He's also taught me that the only way to be more ninja than putting a good stalk on fish is to be still enough to let the fish come to you.

All of this experimentation led Gregg to the egg fly. Now, I'm not suggesting that Gregg invented eggs flies or that he is the only person fishing them for carp. On the contrary, these flies are proven fish takers for many fishermen all over the country. Gregg simply serves to illuminate the most unique characteristic of these flies. Namely, egg flies have the ability to get fish to eat regardless of what or even whether they are eating.

DESCRIPTION

Fish eggs exist anywhere there are fish and are eaten by most species at one time or another. They are found in basically all colors and shapes and have a wide range of sizes. I'd get more specific, but I'm not sure it matters because I don't think carp eat egg flies because they think they are fish eggs.

To be honest, I'm not sure what carp think they are. These flies could easily be mistaken for an egg. They could just as easily fool the fish into thinking they were vegetable matter. I've seen them compared to the bodies of clams that have died and come out of the shell and even to pieces of bread or corn. The fact is, carp might think eggs flies are anything and therein is their effectiveness.

When you have a fly that could look like many different food sources and gets eaten by fish for unexplainable reasons, it is a universal fly. They take tailing fish, shopping fish, and clooping fish. More impressively, fish that are not actively feeding can be induced into eating with more regularity by egg flies than any other pattern. Non-feeding carp are normally terrible targets. Fish that are suspended in the water, motionless, or are slowly moving mid-column just won't eat. If you are armed with an egg fly and an accurate cast, these fish become viable targets. It's really a strange phenomenon that I have never heard adequately explained, but it just works.

PATTERN CHARACTERISTICS

Egg flies are historically tied using a simple packed yarn technique. Yarn is a soft and supple material that holds its shape well in water and sinks slowly. Eggs have a tendency to be opaque in the water, and that effect is something tiers strive for in their egg flies. Everything from varying the material to adding veils is used to create this effect. I don't know how important it really is, but it's better to have it and not need it than to need it and not have it.

Eggs can be pinks, peach, yellow, and cream-colored, but egg flies can range from chartreuse to red. Some flies will incorporate two or more colors to give the illusion of a yolk sack. Remember, you probably aren't trying to tie something that looks exactly like an egg. We don't even know if that's what the fly is being mistaken for. General size, fleshy tones, and sink rate are probably all more important than any particular detail in your fly.

Photo by Elek Erdosy.

PRESENTATION

The general presentation method for egg flies is a dead drift. That is to say, if you are in a current, dead drift the fly to the fish, and if you are in still water, let it sink dead right past the fish's face. It's odd to think of dead drifting a fly in still water, but that is exactly what you are looking for. The fly should slowly descend through the water column with no action at all if you can help it. The vibrancy of the egg flies is usually enough to draw the attention of the fish and get it to eat.

One of the benefits of tying with buoyant egg materials is that you generally get a slow sink rate. That's what you are looking for with this fly. The closer you can get to actually suspending the fly in front of the face of a carp, the better off you are. You'd like your fly to slowly drift within six inches of a carp's mouth and hang there as long as possible.

This near suspension of the fly is vital when fishing to nonfeeding fish. Frankly, these fish are slow to react. They need to notice the fly, decide to start feeding, and then eat the fly. That process can take a second, and if the fly has already passed out of the feeding zone, you're probably not going to get a take. If you can, try getting near enough to the carp to dap the fly in front of them and actually suspend it. The longer you can keep the egg on the dinner plate the better—whether that is on the bottom or mid-column.

Another effective presentation method involves a strike indicator. Carp that are feeding in deeper water are difficult fish. You may only see their tail or even just the bubble trail they are leaving on the bottom. These actively feeding fish would be great targets if only you could tell when they had eaten your fly. That is a difficult task when you can't see the fish's head. An effective solution is one that Gregg uses with regularity. He will cast an egg suspended under a strike indicator in front of a bubble trail made by an actively feeding fish. The indicator should be positioned so the egg is held just off the bottom. The fish will work its way toward the fly, and as it approaches, Gregg will set the hook on the slightest movement. This is a good way to catch carp in deep or turbid situations.

FLY PATTERNS

Cohen's Double Goo Egg

Hook: Gamakatsu L10-2H, size 6

Thread: Hot Orange 210 Denier flat wax nylon

Tail: Krystal flash

Eggs: CCG Flex, colored with sharpie to match a laser dub overdubbing

Veil: White laser dub

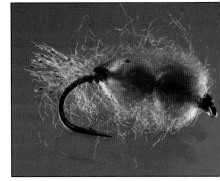

Photo by McTage Tanner.

Erdosy's Carp Spawn

Hook: Tiemco 2457 or equivalent, sizes 6–14

Thread: Danville 70 Denier, matched to color of yarn

Body Material: Orvis Egg Yarn or The Bug Shop Glo Bug Yarn

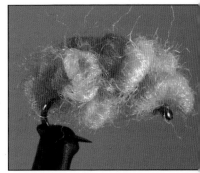

Photo by Tuck Scott.

Gregg's Egg

Hook: Mustad C67S, TMC 105, Dai Riki 155, or equivalent egg style, sizes 6–10

Thread: UTC 140 Denier or equivalent, color to match body

Body: Tightly spun and packed, trimmed, egg yarns or wool/acrylic or similar craft store yarns—Peach, Peachy King, Golden Nugget, Oregon Cheese, White, alone or mottled

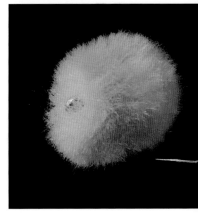

Photo by McTage Tanner.

Cohen's Crystal Meth

Hook: Mustad C49S, size 8
Thread: Danville Flat Waxed
     Nylon 210, Hot Orange
Body: Pearl Diamond Braid

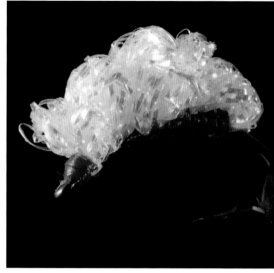

Photo by Tuck Scott.

10
Hybrids

A RECENT PHENOMENON IN CARP FLY DESIGN IS THE emergence of hybrids. There are crayfish patterns that look nymphy and clams that look crayfishy. Most carp flies are impressionistic enough that they could be mistaken for more than one category of food item. The presentation has far more to do with what exactly you are emulating than the fly itself. So most carp flies have characteristics of many different of food items. It gives the angler flexibility and increases the chances the carp will make a mistake.

When designers started tying worms on their soft hackles, they took this notion to a whole different level.

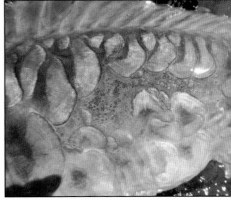

The hybrid concept takes the best parts of other flies and puts them all together in one pattern. The hope is that the carp will see what it wants when it looks at your fly, regardless of what that may be. If a carp is eating worms, this fly will have enough worm elements to get eaten. If it is eating clams, the flies suggest that, too. Nymphs, same. It's an interesting concept, and it works.

Photo by Travis Hammond.

PATTERN CHARACTERISTICS

Regardless of how tasty a fly looks, the carp aren't going to move very far to eat it. By nature, carp in most locations are quite lazy. They will tail and shop and pick prey off the bottom, but it's difficult to entice a carp to move a long way for a fly. That fact can't be overcome by even the most universal of patterns.

For bottom-feeding fish, the base pattern, or pattern onto which the tail is being added, is a nondescript fly. Tiers don't go to the trouble of tying a nice clean crayfish and then add a tail. Instead they start with something such as a soft hackle. That fly alone is suggestive of everything from nymphs to clams to drowned terrestrial insects. Long hackle legs and mottled bodies help give the flies a generally buggy feel. A worm tail is then added to that fly. Once the tail is on the fly, it could be even more things. Maybe it's a worm burrowing under a rock, or maybe it's a long siphon on a clam. The tendency is for these flies to be in the nebulous size 4–10 range, again, where they might be anything. When it's all said and done, tying on a hybrid such as this is almost like fishing five flies at once.

Eggs patterns modified to include worm tails are very versatile.

Photo by Targhee Boss.

When carp are holding in currents or slowly cruising in the middle of the water column, the egg hybrids are more effective. Egg hybrids are egg flies or spawn flies with worm tails protruding from the back. The delicacy and slow sink rate of these flies allow them to be nearly suspended in front of fish anywhere in the water column. This feature alone makes them effective patterns for presenting to fish that are normally marginal targets. Add to that the increased visibility of an egg and tail combination, and you have a deadly fly.

PRESENTATION

Here is where hybrid flies come into their own. The flies themselves have many different characteristics, all suggestive of some type of carp food. It is up to the angler to manipulate the fly so the carp picks up on what it wants to see and ignores the rest. That can be a tricky business. The key with hybrid flies is to vary your presentation rather than change flies.

With the bottom-fished hybrids, the idea is to let the carp see what they want to see or rather to cause them to see what you want them to see. To do this, you still have to know your water and the major forage sources. You want to know how the natural prey acts in the water so you can present the fly accordingly.

If nymphs seem to be on the menu, use the Drag-and-Drop presentation method or a slow crawl along the bottom to make the fly look like a fleeing nymph. If they are eating clams or worms, then let the fly sit. Crayfish require small strips. It all comes down to seeing the hybrid the way you hope a carp would. Should it look like a clam with a long siphon sticking out? Is it a worm sticking out from under a pebble? Are you trying to show the

Modifying your presentation allows a hybrid pattern to be any number of different possible food organisms.

Photo by John "Montana" Bartlett.

carp a crawling nymph? Whatever the forage item, the hybrid can give that impression if you present it correctly.

The egg hybrids are more straightforward. Presenting them is much like presenting an egg fly or an unweighted worm fly. You want to find a way to get the fly to stay in the carp's feeding zone for as long as possible with a dead drift. In current, find the position that will allow the fly to drift along naturally right into the fish's face. When on still water, you will want to cast beyond the fish and drag the fly across the top—again the Drag-and-Drop presentation—and then let it settle through the water in front of your carp. The longer the fly hangs within a few inches of the carp's mouth the better. If you can dap them with these flies, by all means, do it.

Photo by Targhee Boss.

FLY PATTERNS

Montana Hybrid—John "Montana" Bartlett

Hook: CarpPro Gaper, size 6 or 8
Weight: Dumbbell eyes to size and color for weight and flash as needed
Body: Peacock chenille body
Tail: Claret chenille tail
Hackle: Yellow pheasant hackle

Photo by McTage Tanner.

Catch's Wabbit Worm—Eric Beebe

Hook: Dai-Riki #810, size 4
Thread: Danville 210 Denier black
Eyes: Dazzle Dumbbell eyes
Tail: Red Standard Ultra Chenille
Body: Black Rabbit in a dubbing loop
Legs: Olive Flexi Legs

Photo by Tuck Scott.

Hammond's Craw-brid—Travis Hammond

Hook: Gamakatsu SL45, size 6–8
Thread: Olive or rust brown
Weight: Black brass dumbbell eyes and lead wire wrapped 2/3 down the shank
Split tail: Speckled olive or speckled orange medium Centipede Legs or Tarantu-Leggs
Worm Tail: Wine, claret, or orange Ultra Chenille Standard
Body: Olive or rust brown Free Range dubbing or dubbing of choice
Hackle: Olive or rust brown CDC
Collar Legs: Olive or fire tip pumpkin or orange Sili Legs

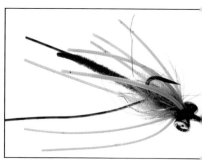

Photo by McTage Tanner.

Travis' Tournament Fly

Hook: Black Gamakatsu C14S, size 6

Thread: Black

Tail: Two pieces of round, orange and black striped rubber legs, tied in a V shape

Weight: Spirit River nickel I-balz, size 3/16 or 5/32

Hackle: Soft grizzly hackle palmered from tail to eyes

Body: Teased black angora goat hair rope made from a dubbing loop

Photo by McTage Tanner.

McTage's McLuvin'—McTage Tanner

Hook: Tiemco 2457 caddis, size 8

Thread: 140 Denier Ultra-Thread, burnt orange

Bead: 3.25 mm brass, black

Eyes: Bead chain #6, stainless

Tail: Micro-pine squirrel, brown

Body: Nymph Dubbing, rust brown

Collar: Small Hungarian Partridge, brown

Head: UV Dub, pink shrimp

Photo by McTage Tanner.

McTage's Sculpin Head McLuvin'— McTage Tanner

Hook: CarpPro Gaper, size 6

Head: Fly-Men Sculpin Helment, mini olive

Thread: 140 Denier Ultra-Thread, any color

Tail: Micro-pine squirrel zonker, sculpin olive

Body: Spirit River UV2 Dubbing, scud shrimp olive

Collar: Palmered micro-pine squirrel zonker, sculpin olive

Photo by McTage Tanner.

Gregg's Egg Worm—Gregg Martin

Hook: Mustad C67S, TMC 105, Dai Riki 155 or equivalent egg style, sizes 8–10

Bead: ⅛" tungsten gold

Tail: Standard vernille, tan, ¾–1"

Body: Tightly spun and packed, trimmed, egg yarns, Peach, Golden Nugget, Peachy King, Oregon Cheese, alone or mottled

Photo by McTage Tanner.

Majcher's Egg Sucking Worm—Nolan Majcher

Hook: Dai-Riki 135, size 12

Thread: 6/0 red UNI-thread

Tail: Ultra Chenille, tan, brown, or orange

Eyes: Bead chain

Body: McFly Foam, yellow, white, or orange

Photo by McTage Tanner.

Majcher's Worm Spawn—Nolan Majcher

Hook: Daiichi 1120, size 12–16

Bead: ⅛" black or brass

Thread: 6/0 red UNI-thread

Body: Glo Bug Yarn, egg

Tail: Ultra Chenille, red, tan, orange, or brown

Photo by McTage Tanner.

A Final Note

IF THERE IS ONE THOUGHT THAT I HAVE TRIED TO emphasize over the last many pages, it is this: the most important information that someone attempting to catch carp on the fly needs is an understanding of what the carp are eating. We all went through a period of time early in our fly fishing where we didn't know what we were doing. We used the wrong flies, gave poor presentations, and fished the wrong water. With most species, there were enough individual fish willing to make mistakes to keep our interest. As we learned, we improved and began to do things better; we started to catch more and smarter fish. Carp seem so difficult to beginners because few of them make mistakes. The wrong fly, presentation, or fish will so rarely draw a strike that it begins to feel hopeless. It isn't. People all over the United States are catching these difficult fish with regularity. The funny thing is that very few of them do it the same way.

As you read or talk to carp anglers, you are sure to get conflicting information. Some will tell you it's larger flies stripped actively. Others will tell you it's tiny flies fished without any action and everything in between. The underlying theme that any fly fishermen can miss in all this conflicting information is simple: these people devised methods that work well on their waters because it gives their local carp what they want. In other words, it's not the methods they have devised that are important. It's realizing that methods and flies that work one place may not work somewhere else.

Understanding your forage answers almost every question that you need to get started. It will tell you what size and profile your fly should be. It will give you a good idea of how to present and manipulate that fly. And it will let you know which fish are good targets and which aren't. Show a feeding fish a fly that looks and moves like their prey, and fly fishing carp will get much easier.